# A TASTE OF THE
# GREEK
# ISLANDS

## Pamela Westland

*Special cookery photography by Derek St Romaine*

CHARLES LETTS
*Letts*
of London®
FOUNDED 1796

TO ANNA

All weights and measurements are given in both
metric and Imperial equivalents; use one system or
the other – not a combination of the two.

First published in 1992
by Charles Letts & Co Ltd
Letts of London House,
Parkgate Road,
London SW11 4NQ

Conceived and designed by
Jonathan Andrews Editions

Editor: Lydia Darbyshire
Cookery photography: Derek St Romaine
Home economist: Kate Gaselee
Food Stylist: Dawn St Romaine

A CIP catalogue record for this book is available from
the British Library

'Letts' is a registered trademark of
Charles Letts & Co Limited

ISBN 1 85238 152 3

Typeset by XL Publishing Services, Nairn
Printed in Hong Kong by
Regent Publishing Services Ltd.

# Contents

Introduction 7

1 The Peloponnese and
Saronic Gulf 11

2 The Cyclades 27

3 The Dodecanese 43

4 Crete 59

5 The Northeast Aegean 79

6 Evia and the Sporades 95

7 Corfu and Ionia 111

A Taste of Greek Wines 129

Vocabulary 140

Acknowledgements 141

Index 142

# Introduction

Tender, tasty young octopus simmered in red wine and enjoyed close to the archaeological splendours of ancient Corinth; filo pastry pies, oozing with creamy cheese and fresh herbs, bought at the baker's morning after morning on Siphnos; tuna fish steaks served with the most pungent of garlic sauces at a harbourside taverna on Rhodes; baby lamb cutlets cooked 'bandit style' in paper parcels, a welcome meal at the beginning of a long, long trek on Crete; a picnic of lamb and macaroni pie, *pastitsio*, on a tree-fringed beach on Thassos; plump, round figs cooked in honey and wine just where they grow, in a hillside village on Evia; strawberries soaked in icing sugar and ouzo, a refreshing climax to the Easter Day celebrations in an olive grove on Corfu – for me, the food of the Greek islands is inextricably linked, in a long chain of delectable memories, with the history, the scenery and, most of all, the warmth and generosity of the people.

Greek island cooking has a long and proud tradition. Owing nothing to fad, fashion or fancy, it makes the very best of the seasonal produce of the land and sea and, as it has done for centuries, makes sensible provision for the long, hard winters. Food that is in plentiful local supply – it may be fish and seafood, meat, poultry and game, or fruit and vegetables – is firmly planted in the regional cuisine and will be enjoyed to the full.

Take artichokes, for example. Drive through field upon field bristling with the tall, stately silvery-grey spikes of globe artichoke plants – in Crete, it could be – and you may be sure that you will be offered them in every possible delicious way. Pickled artichokes (winter provisions, remember) will be offered as an appetizer and a digestive, in mixed salads and as a garnish; the youngest and most tender of the vegetables, marinated briefly in wine, will be served raw, as a first course; more mature ones, cooked to a yielding succulence, will be filled with, variously, minced meat, prawns, or rice and herbs – there is no end to the flavour combinations and ingenuity of on-the-spot cuisine.

## FISH AND SEAFOOD

Think of a Greek island and you may think first, perhaps, of a harbourside scene, colourful fishing boats moored up alongside, the fishermen busy coiling their nets and unloading boxes of glinting, gleaming and often unrecognizable fish. Or of the unmistakable sound of a battered motor vehicle making its way from village to village, with the vendor loudly – and sometimes to a musical accompaniment – proclaiming his wares and offering those same boxes of morning-fresh fish to customers all over the island. Taking a quite

*Opposite: A study in high texture and understated colour, the castle in Paroikia, Paros. Below: A moment of triumph as red mullet, or* barbounia, *is landed – one of the most prized fish in the islands.*

different perspective, you might see yourself in a hired boat, battling with the often hostile elements to secure your own hard-won sea harvest or, in a more tranquil and leisurely vein, fishing in rock pools or from the end of a jetty. No problem! If you are not 'self catering', it is the accepted thing to take your catch to a taverna and ask the proprietor to cook it for you, for a small fee, as part of your meal.

To anyone who is not part of the Greek fishing fraternity, it can seem that a lifetime's study is needed to identify the incredible variety of fish and seafood on offer, and that is just what makes eating in Greece such an exciting experience. You could, I am sure, enjoy a different species of fish – sardines or scorpion-fish, mackerel or mullet – cooked in a different way and served with a different sauce on every day of the year, without fear of repetition.

The recipes I have chosen are representative of those you might sample around the islands. They range from a homely sardine omelette on Lesbos to an artistic presentation of fish mayonnaise on

neighbouring Lemnos, from the traditional one-pot mixed fish soup, *kakavia*, of Paros to the sophisticated version of baked sea bream in a spicy sauce that is a feature of Spetsai.

If you are unable to obtain any of the fish specified in the recipes, substitute the closest you can find, and use any other white or oily fish that your fishmonger has, relying on the other ingredients – the olive oil, ripe tomatoes, herbs, spices and lemon juice – to give your cooking the authentic flavour of the islands.

## MEAT, POULTRY AND GAME

No matter how many times you are held up on a lonely mountain road by sheep or goats ambling across the way, nor how loud the cacophony of farmyard cockerels that disturbs you in the morning, nor how many khaki-clad sportsmen you encounter relaxing in a *kafenion* in the shooting

---

### The Café Society

You can't travel far in Greece without beginning to appreciate the role played by the *kafenion*, the coffee shop, in the local culture. Two rickety cane-bottomed chairs and a metal table on the pavement outside a small, dimly lit room may be all it takes to encourage two of the locals to order a coffee, or maybe an ouzo, and to reach for the backgammon board.

The *kafenion* is very much a male domain, a cross between a working-men's club and a pub, where customers can – some do – sit for half a day with a single drink. Greek women do not normally invade this most masculine of strongholds, although visiting females – I write from years of experience –

are made genially welcome and need not feel at all out of place. No, it doesn't seem fair!

Come to think of it, the only time I have seen a group of Greek women in a village *kafenion* was in Kalamitsi, to the west of Lefkas, where the coffee shop doubles as a council office, and an official comes once a week to pay out the pensions. Even so, the women, in their distinctive brown costumes, sat discreetly on the steps outside, awaiting their turn to be asked to cross the threshold.

The bill of fare, which may be written up on a blackboard outside the shop, is often severely limited, stopping short at coffee, spirits and soft drinks and, in many cases, not even extending to beer.

Some *kafenions* do have well-stocked ice-cream cabinets outside, but don't expect a meal or even a snack – that's not what coffee shops are there for, although, as I have indicated elsewhere, many's the time a friendly proprietor has come to the rescue with a tin of sardines and a tomato or brought out a little delicacy from his wife's larder. But such kindness is typically Greek.

season, it is never tactful to take meat, poultry and game for granted, at least in Greek island homes. I have found that it is treated by many of the local people with a mixture of respect and something verging on reverence, an attitude that goes back to the days when religious fasting was even more rigorously observed than it is now and when meat was, for a large majority of families, a rarely affordable luxury. And even now it can be expensive. I was astonished to find that a rabbit I bought on one of the islands to test a recipe cost more than five times as much as it would at home – and the field outside our cottage was teeming with them at the time.

Lamb is, of course, by far the most popular and readily available meat: spit-roast whole in celebration of Easter, weddings and other festive occasions; cooked in a casserole with vegetables and fruit (lemons or quinces, for example); barbecued over glowing coals outside many a welcoming taverna; layered with vegetables and pasta, cheese and yoghurt to make a brown and bubbling gratinated dish; and minced and mixed with rice to fill baked aubergines, courgettes and tomatoes. On some islands goat takes precedence; enjoy it when you can. It has a stronger flavour than lamb – somewhat similar to that of mutton – and it takes a little longer to cook. If you can buy goat at home, perhaps in a Greek or Asian butcher's, you can, with the appropriate adjustment to cooking times, substitute it in the lamb recipes that follow.

I have always had a special regard for the Greek ways of cooking chicken, whether it is an old boiling fowl that has been scratching around in the farmyard for many a long day or a sprightly young chicken that needs the minimum of culinary disguise. And I have many grateful memories of island interludes when I have been allowed to help cook the family meal, combining chicken with the crunch of pistachios or the 'bite' of olives, imparting the flavour of cinnamon or serving the bird with a walnut sauce. But I find that my attitude to complementary flavours and textures is not always reciprocated. When young Greek friends were staying with us recently, I thought they would like to try roast chicken English style, with apple and raisin stuffing and home-made redcurrant jelly. You learn something every day. Georgia wasted no time in advising me that 'Greeks never eat jam with their meat, Pamela'!

# VEGETABLES AND FRUIT

Anyone who appreciates vegetables that are markedly undercooked will find a spiritual home in some of the islands; when, that is, they can find vegetables on the menu at all. It is a constant source of mystery to me that so many taverna proprietors put all their efforts into producing a perfectly balanced Greek country salad, *horiatikisalata*, of lettuce, peppers, cucumber, onions, tomatoes and feta cheese yet offer such a poor selection of vegetables.

But what a delight they are when you do find them! I think back with pleasure to a surprise salad of raw baby broad beans served with feta and onion wedges as *mezethakia* with lunch-time drinks at a café in Crete; only-just-cooked wild green leaves drizzled with olive oil and lemon juice, which are equally good whether they are served hot or cold; a medley of crisp, colourful vegetables in tangy golden egg and lemon sauce, *avgolemono*; and young okra in lightly spiced tomato sauce – each dish so good that it merits a course to itself.

If vegetables can sometimes seem to be the hidden assets of the islands, the fruit harvests mark the comings and goings of the seasons as surely as any calendar. The hustle and bustle as the vivid citrus fruit crops are harvested in the Argolid, the massive green-on-green striped watermelons of Eleia, the mulberries of Andros, mellow golden quinces on Karpathos, pomegranates on Rhodes, bananas on Crete, pears on Ikaria, figs on Evia, kumquats on Corfu, and the vines that paint so many of the islands in shades that turn from soft gold to deep purple – there is no mistaking the importance of fruit in the economy and cuisine of the islands. Flipping through my recipe notebook, I have shared with you island specialities ranging from apples poached in wine to pomegranate seeds in syrup, from honey-coated baked quinces to bitter-sweet grape juice paste.

Perhaps most significant of all is the recipe for preserved kumquats, just one example of a 'spoon sweet' that is traditionally offered to visitors as a symbol of Greek hospitality and a sign of welcome. That simple custom, which you will encounter from Thassos in the north to Crete in the south, sums up the warmth and friendliness of a people and, for me, epitomizes the true joy of the Greek islands.

# CHAPTER 1

# The Peloponnese and Saronic Gulf

What place, you might reasonably ask, has the Peloponnese in a book on the Greek Islands? Well, counsel for the defence points out, Peloponnisos was an island once, and in ancient times it was known as the Island of Pelops. The peninsula, shaped like an outstretched hand, is separated from the rest of mainland Greece by a narrow canal – the construction of which defeated Emperor Nero's finest engineers – and linked to it by a road bridge on the fast route from Athens to Corinth. This large region, which covers some 21,500 square kilometres (more than 8,000 square miles) and is divided into seven prefectures, has, I promise you, all the 'feel' of an island. Not only that, it presents a fascinating kaleidoscope of so much of the history and pre-history – Mycenae, Olympia, Epidavros – sights and sounds, food and wines that Greece has to offer. And some surprises.

Driving through Messinia, home of the succulent Kalamata olive, we had to agree with Euripides who described it as 'a land of fair fruit-age. . . abounding in pasturage'. Shepherds' huts, like pieces carefully positioned on a chess board, dot the fields, which are separated by mellow stone walls. Sheep amble nonchalantly in what passes for a road, and there, by a stream, is an old lady washing wool, swishing it back and forth in the icy water. Only it isn't wool. On closer inspection, it turns out to be skeins of sheeps' intestines wound round the end of a stick and destined to make the local version of *kokoretsi*, that waste-not, want-not sausage-on-a-skewer. The lady

said she cooked it slowly, over a wood fire in her outside kitchen, after which, as I can testify from experience, it would be a great deal tastier than it looked.

Mani, in the south of the region, has a strangely sombre air, in spite of the patchwork fields of wild

*Opposite: Monemvassia, one of the country's hidden treasures, is built into the seaward side of a massive rock. Below: Lemons, a major crop, are used extensively in the local cuisine.*

flowers and sunny banks of yellow broom. The houses, many of them now animal shelters, are imposing, four-square, grey-stone towers, like so many Norman keeps.

An old man with a donkey ambles by, and four one-month-old kids peer inquisitively out of the saddle-bags. A bank of wild asparagus brings an unexpected lushness to the scene. And there, by the roadside, an unconcerned traveller is cooking the spears on a gas burner, surely the most enterprising picnic ever.

The Saronic Gulf islands, which form an arc from Piraeus around the shores of the Argolid, are different again, and each one is different from the next: Salamis, closest to Athens, opens up the prospect of lazy taverna meals among thick pine forests; Aegina, prized for the magnificent Temple of Aphaia Athene, is splashed petal-pink with pistachio blossom; and Poros, offshore from the Peloponnese and Lemonodassos, is noted for its light-as-air doughnuts, best enjoyed at dusk as the fishermen set out in the convoys of *gri-gri* boats. Hydra, a largely barren island noted for its lack of motor transport, has an elegant if faded charm and a welcoming wave of waterside cafés, while on neighbouring Spetsai, or Spetses, the fashionable pastry shops are the big temptation, and fish in unusually spicy sauces is the local speciality.

---

# COUNTRY BEAN SOUP

## *Fasolia soupa*

Holidaying along the lovely Messinian coast or sauntering through the richly fertile plains, one may not realize quite how high and remote some of the mountain villages are nor how cold it can be in winter. We first saw the breathtaking Temple of Apollo at Bassae – an architectural match for the Parthenon – in a stinging snowstorm. Lucky, then, that thick, spicy bean soup is a local speciality.

### SERVES 6

*4 tbsp olive oil*
*2 stalks celery, thickly sliced*
*1 medium onion, thickly sliced*
*1 tsp cumin seed, crushed*
*100g (4oz) canned tomatoes*
*1 tbsp tomato purée*
*350g (12oz) haricot beans, soaked overnight and drained*
*125g (5oz) yellow split peas, washed and drained*
*1·5 litres (2½) pints meat stock or water*
*1 tbsp lemon juice*
*salt and black pepper*
*2 tbsp chopped parsley*

Heat the oil in a large pan and fry the celery and onion over medium heat until the onion is transparent. Stir in the crushed cumin seed and cook for 1 minute. Add the tomatoes, tomato purée, haricot beans and split peas and stir well. Pour on the stock or water and cover the pan.

Bring to the boil and fast-boil for at least 10 minutes. Skim off any foam that has risen to the top. Lower the heat and simmer for 1–1¼ hours until the haricot beans are tender and the split peas have thickened the soup.

Add the lemon juice. Season with salt and pepper and stir in the parsley.

# OCTOPUS IN RED WINE

## *Htapothi krasato*

After a morning spent in the archaeological majesty of ancient Corinth, backed impressively by rocky peaks and surrounded by vines, oleander, almond and citrus trees, it was time for lunch. Several bumpy tracks later and after a chat with a lady dividing her attention between her umbrella, her crochet and her goat, we came across a taverna offering – the owner apologized – only one dish of the day. It was this.

## SERVES 4–6

*1kg (2¼lb) young octopus*
*8 tbsp olive oil*
*350g (12oz) small onions or shallots*
*150ml (¼ pint) red wine*
*6 tbsp red wine vinegar*
*225g (8oz) canned tomatoes, roughly chopped*
*2 tbsp tomato purée*
*4 bay leaves*
*2 tsp dried oregano*
*black pepper*
*2 tbsp chopped parsley*

First clean the octopus. Pull off the tentacles, remove and discard the intestines and the ink sac, the eyes and the beak. Skin the octopus and wash and scrub it thoroughly to remove any traces of sand. Cut it into 4–5cm (1½–2in) pieces and put it into a saucepan over medium heat to release the liquid. Stir the octopus until this liquid has evaporated.

Pour on the oil and stir the octopus to seal it on all sides. Add the whole onions and cook them, stirring once or twice, until they colour slightly.

Add the wine, the vinegar, tomatoes, tomato purée, bay leaves, oregano and several grindings of pepper. Stir well, cover the pan and simmer very gently for 1–1 ¼ hours, checking from time to time that the sauce has not dried out. If it does – and this would only happen if the heat were too high – add a little more wine or water. The octopus is cooked when it can be easily pierced with a skewer.

The sauce should be thick, like a runny paste. If any of the liquid separates, remove the lid from the pan, slightly increase the heat and stir until some of the liquid evaporates and the sauce thickens. Discard the bay leaves and stir in the parsley. Taste the sauce and adjust the seasoning if necessary.

Serve, if you like, with rice and a salad. A Greek essential is country bread to mop up the sauce.

---

# VINE LEAF PARCELS

*Dolmadakia me rizi*

Around the mountainous region of Corinth the yellow soil is dry and ideally suited to the cultivation of grapes, a crop that paints the landscape for miles on end. Some of the harvest goes to the wineries to make the well-known Nemean wine – also known as Heracles' blood – but far, far more is left to dry on the vine to become tightly packed bunches of sun-ripened currants, the principal and centuries-old export of the region.

This traditional *meze*, or snack dish, uses them in a delightful way.

## MAKES ABOUT 30 PARCELS

*4 tbsp olive oil*
*2 medium onions, finely chopped*
*50g (2oz) long-grain rice, washed and drained*
*salt and black pepper*
*juice of 2 lemons*
*1 tbsp honey*
*2 tbsp currants*
*1tbsp pine kernels*
*400g (14oz) can vine leaves, washed, drained and dried. (If you use fresh vine leaves, blanch them in boiling water for 1 minute)*

Heat 3 tbsp of the oil in a large frying-pan and fry the onions until they are transparent. Add the rice and stir to coat the grains thoroughly with oil. Pour on 150ml (¼ pint) water, season with salt and pepper and add the juice of 1 lemon and the honey. Stir well, cover and simmer for 15–20 minutes until the rice is tender and has absorbed the liquid. If, once the rice is cooked, there is any excess liquid, increase the heat slightly and uncover the pan until it evaporates.

Stir in the currants and pine kernels and turn the filling into a bowl. Set aside to cool.

Arrange five or six vine leaves to cover the base of the cleaned pan.

To fill the vine leaves, place each one, shiny side down, on the work surface. Place a dessertspoonful of the filling in the centre and fold over the stalk end of the leaf to cover it. Fold over each side, and then roll up the leaf from the stalk end to form a parcel and completely enclose the filling. Place the parcels, join side down, in a single layer in the pan.

Mix together the remaining oil and lemon juice with 6 tbsp water and pour over the parcels. Cover the pan and simmer for about 45 minutes. Check once or twice that the liquid has not dried out. If it has, add a little more water.

Uncover the pan and leave the parcels to cool.

Serve them, with yoghurt, as a first course or as a snack with drinks.

## LOBSTER IN OIL AND LEMON DRESSING

*Astakos me saltsa latholemono*

The horseshoe-shaped harbour of Hydra, with its stage-set backdrop of elegant but largely deserted sea captains' houses, is the perfect setting in which to indulge in that ultimate holiday luxury, spiny lobster – even though it seems to be work-a-day fare on the island.

To make the most of such seeming extravagance back at home and to bring out the full flavour of the seafood, the secret is to poach it not just in water but in a well-flavoured stock.

### SERVES 2

*1 spiny lobster, about 1kg (2¼ lb)*
*100ml (4fl oz) olive oil*
*3 tbsp lemon juice*
*a pinch of mustard powder*
*salt and black pepper*
*2 tsp chopped parsley*
*lemon wedges, to serve*

### BOUILLON
*3 stalks celery, thickly sliced*
*2 medium carrots, thickly sliced*
*1 medium onion, quartered*
*2 large cloves garlic, sliced*
*1 lemon, quartered*
*salt and black pepper*

Put the bouillon ingredients and the lobster into a large pan and pour on enough water to cover. Bring to the boil and cover the pan. Simmer for 25–30 minutes. Drain and reserve the bouillon – it's a perfect base for fish soup – and set aside the lobster to cool.

Split the lobster in half lengthways. Clean it by removing the stomach, gills and intestine, which runs along the tail, then wash and dry thoroughly. Pierce the lobster flesh all over with a fine skewer to allow the dressing to penetrate.

Mix together the oil, lemon juice and mustard and season with salt and pepper.

Grill the lobster under medium heat, shell side up, for 3–4 minutes. Turn the lobster, brush the

*Pages 14–15: Vine Leaf Parcels; recipe on page 13.*

flesh liberally with the oil and lemon mixture and grill for a further 8–10 minutes, brushing frequently with more of the dressing. Sprinkle with the parsley and serve hot, with lemon wedges.

A chilled mixed salad and thick slices of rough, country bread are the traditional accompaniments.

---

## LAMB COOKED WITH LEMONS

*Arni lemonato*

As soon as I set foot in Kalavrita, a rebuilt mountainside town in the northern Peloponnese, my nose – which is well trained, I have to admit – guided me to the most evocative back-street baker's shop, its shelves overflowing with country breads representing centuries of the region's proud heritage. Call it instinct that led on to a lovely landlady a few doors away who just happened to be cooking this most tangy and unusual of lamb dishes.

### SERVES 4

*5 tbsp olive oil*
*1kg (2¼ lb) lamb, cut from the shoulder and cubed*
*2 medium onions, sliced*
*2 tsp dried oregano*
*300ml (½ pint) light stock or water*
*juice of 1 lemon*
*2 lemons, quartered*
*salt and black pepper*
*40g (1½ oz) butter*
*175g (6oz) mushrooms, halved or sliced*
*1 tbsp chopped parsley*
*lemon wedges, to serve (optional)*

Heat the oil in a saucepan and, depending on its circumference, fry the meat in one or two batches over medium heat, stirring until it is lightly coloured on all sides. Remove the meat with a draining spoon and fry the onion until it is transparent.

Return the lamb to the pan, stir in the oregano and pour on the stock or water. Add the lemon juice and the quartered lemons and season with salt and pepper.

Cover, and simmer slowly for 1¼–1½ hours until the meat is tender.

Just before the end of the cooking time, melt the butter in a small pan and fry the mushrooms over medium heat for 3–4 minutes.

Remove the lemon quarters from the pan and stir in the mushrooms. Simmer for a further 5–10 minutes for the flavours to blend. Taste the sauce and adjust the seasoning if necessary. Sprinkle with the chopped parsley and serve with lemon wedges if you wish.

Our dish was brought to the table with a huge bowl of plain boiled, waxy potatoes, peeled and cut, in the Greek way, in quarters lengthways, and a plaited loaf topped with golden sesame seeds.

# RED MULLET WITH EGG AND LEMON SAUCE

*Barbounia avgolemono*

Red mullet, that coral-red fish with the sparkling scales, crops up all over Greece and the islands. It's the usually expensive treat that visitors quickly come to enjoy – though not, as I learned to my discomfort, when they are encouraged to down the fish fisherman-style, head first, bones and all!

This much more elegant presentation was served to us just outside Monemvassia, that almost deserted Byzantine city that nestles in the shelter of a massive rocky promontory on the eastern coast of Laconia.

## SERVES 4

*flour for dusting*
*salt and black pepper*
*1 tsp dried thyme*
*4 red mullet, cleaned, washed and dried*
*olive oil, for shallow frying*
*lemon wedges, to serve*

### SAUCE
*300ml (½ pint) fish stock (see below)*
*1 tbsp cornflour*
*2 egg yolks*
*2 tbsp lemon juice*
*salt and black pepper*

### FISH STOCK
*about 350g (12oz) fish trimmings*
*(heads, tails and fins from the fishmonger)*
*1 medium onion, quartered*
*1 medium carrot, quartered*
*1 stalk celery, thickly sliced*
*2 stalks parsley*

Begin by making the stock. Wash the fish trimmings and put them in a saucepan with the other ingredients and about 600ml (1 pint) water. Bring to the boil, skim off any foam that rises to the surface, cover the pan and set at a fast simmer for about 45 minutes. Strain and measure the stock and discard the flavouring ingredients. (You can, of course, make the stock in larger quantities and freeze some for future use.)

To make the sauce, pour the measured stock into a pan and heat it to just below boiling point. Mix the cornflour to a smooth, runny paste with a little cold water and stir in a little of the hot stock. Pour the cornflour mixture into the stock and stir continuously over a low heat for 5–10 minutes, until the sauce thickens.

Beat the egg yolks in a bowl and beat in the lemon juice. Pour on a little of the hot sauce, then add the egg mixture to the sauce in the pan. Season with salt and pepper and stir continuously over low heat until the sauce is thick enough to coat the back of the spoon. It is most important that the sauce is not allowed to boil – eggs just long to curdle.

Press a piece of greaseproof paper on to the surface of the sauce and keep it hot while you cook the fish.

Season the flour with salt, pepper and thyme. Toss the fish thoroughly in the flour and shake off any excess. Heat the oil in a large, heavy, flat-bottomed frying-pan until it just begins to smoke – the Greeks are much braver about turning on the heat than we normally are.

Quickly fry the fish for 3–4 minutes on each side, until the coating is golden brown and the flesh firm. Serve piping hot – even if the Greeks don't – garnished with lemon wedges. Serve the sauce separately.

Top: Towering above their neighbours – the distinctive stone-
built houses of Mani, in the southwest of the region. Above:
The water-melon boat plies its wares around the islands, here
at Aegina. Slices of the sunset-coloured fruit are sold from
street stalls. Right: Baked Sea Bream; recipe on page 20.

## BAKED SEA BREAM

*Synagritha sto fourno*

Spetsai was known to the ancients as the 'pine-clad isle' – rightly, since two-thirds of the land is said to be covered by those blue-green, swaying and shimmering trees, which, to those who know their wines, promises well for a local brand of retsina. And, chilled and pale honey-gold, it is the perfect accompaniment for the island's own culinary speciality, baked fish in a rich, herby sauce.

### SERVES 6

*1 sea bream or other whole fish,*
*about 1·5kg (3½ lb), cleaned, gutted and washed*
*juice of 1 lemon*
*salt and black pepper*
*2 sprigs rosemary*
*100ml (4fl oz) olive oil*
*1 medium onion, chopped*
*2 cloves garlic, finely chopped*
*225g (8oz) canned tomatoes, chopped*
*2 tbsp tomato purée*
*100ml (4fl oz) white wine*
*2 tbsp white wine vinegar*
*4 tbsp chopped parsley*
*8 tbsp dried breadcrumbs*
*75g (3oz) feta cheese, crumbled*

Sprinkle the fish inside and out with lemon juice and season with salt and pepper. Tuck the rosemary sprigs inside the fish.

Heat about 4 tbsp of the oil in a saucepan and fry the onion over medium heat until it is transparent. Stir in the remaining oil, the garlic, tomatoes, tomato purée, wine, vinegar and parsley and mix well. Season with salt and pepper and bring the sauce to the boil.

Pour half the sauce into a shallow dish or roasting pan and place the fish on top. Cover it with the remaining sauce and sprinkle on the breadcrumbs.

Bake the fish, uncovered, in the oven at 190°C (375°F/Gas 5) for 35–40 minutes until it is firm.

Just before serving, sprinkle on the crumbled cheese.

## ROAST CHICKEN WITH PISTACHIOS

*Kotopoulo yemisto me fistikia*

The efficient way to travel to Aegina is by hydrofoil, a mere 35 minutes across the Saronic Gulf from the mainland; the memorable way is by caique, the passengers jostling for space and competing for the soundwaves with crate piled upon crate of noisy chickens. Arrive at pistachio-blossom time – pistachio nuts are the main agricultural product on the island – and the landscape is an artist's paradise.

This recipe, served to us in a way-off-the-beaten-track farmhouse, deliciously combines these two elements.

### SERVES 6

*1 oven-ready roasting chicken, 1·5–2kg*
*(3½–4½ lb)*
*juice of 2 lemons*
*salt and black pepper*
*750g (1½ lb) potatoes, quartered lengthways*
*100ml (4fl oz) olive oil*
*1 tbsp dried thyme*
*lemon wedges, to serve*

### STUFFING
*4 tbsp olive oil*
*1 medium onion, chopped*
*75g (3oz) long-grain rice, washed and drained*
*200ml (6fl oz) hot water*
*100g (4oz) pistachios, chopped*
*grated rind and juice of 1 lemon*
*salt and black pepper*
*2 tsp dried thyme*

First make the stuffing. Heat the oil in a saucepan and fry the onion over medium heat until it is transparent but not browned. Stir in the rice to coat it thoroughly with oil. Add the water, stir well and simmer for 5–8 minutes, until the rice begins to soften. Add a little more hot water if the mixture dries out too quickly.

Remove the pan from the heat and stir in the nuts, lemon rind and juice and season with salt, pepper and thyme. (Our hostess used dried thyme flowers, which have a heavenly aroma, but sadly they are not readily available outside Greece.) Set aside to cool.

Wash and dry the chicken inside and out. Pack

the cooled stuffing into the cavity and secure the opening with a small skewer. Rub the chicken with lemon juice and season it on all sides with salt and pepper. Place the chicken in a roasting pan – those lovely round aluminium ones are ideal – and arrange the potatoes around it. Pour the olive oil over the chicken and potatoes and sprinkle with thyme – again, our hostess used thyme flowers. Pour 150ml (¼ pint) water around the bird and season the potatoes with salt and pepper.

Cook in the oven at 200°C (400°F/Gas 6) for about 1½ hours, turning the chicken over once and basting the potatoes several times with the liquid. Check that the chicken is cooked by piercing the thick part of a leg with a skewer. The juices should be clear, not pink.

Serve the chicken on a warm dish, surrounded by the potatoes and lemon wedges. Lightly cooked spinach tossed in oil and lemon juice is a good accompaniment.

## The Baker's

The place of the bakery in Greek culture is summed up in the use of the single word *fournos*, which means both bake-house and oven, for in many villages until very recent times the baker's oven was shared by every household in the community. Even now, it is a familiar and tantalizing sight to see women walking to and from the baker's carrying – always on their heads – a tray of loaves for the family, a dish of corn-fed chicken surrounded by garden vegetables, a casserole of lamb or goat simmered with tomatoes, or a selection of stuffed vegetables.

Bakers have to be versatile cooks. It is left to them, with explicit instructions, to turn and baste the meat, to add vegetables near the end of the cooking time, or to add just the right amount of water – rain water for preference – to a casserole.

Most Greek bread is close-textured, rather heavy (I make absolutely no criticism of that) and a rich cream colour, the product of unbleached flour. The most familiar shape, what might be termed the standard loaf, is a large round, slightly domed in the centre, in the way of my school panama hat. The loaf is usually cut across in thick slices, and then in half, to give unpretentious and satisfying chunks. Different islands have their own traditional loaf shapes – thick, substantial rings, plaits, twists and knots, star shapes and others, with or without a crunchy topping of sesame seeds.

Wholemeal bread hasn't really 'caught on' commercially, but I do have experience of a whole-grain loaf baked by a Cretan farmer who invited us to a meal. The bread was soaked in water for several minutes, squeeze-dried and sprinkled with oil and pepper as an appetizer, to enjoy – if that is the word – with an ouzo. And then it cropped up again at lunch, in pieces just the right size to be used as tools to scoop up the gravy.

By contrast, some families, and indeed some bakers, make a light and lovely bread that is a close relation to the French *brioche*, a high-rise loaf made with egg yolks. This slightly sweetened bread, known as *artos*, is the kind offered to churchgoers on saints' days and other religious festivals, when the priest blesses the loaf and hands a celebratory piece to allcomers.

The pinnacle of the baker's art is reached with the bread he bakes for another celebration, that of a Greek Orthodox wedding. These wedding breads, elaborately decorated with raised fruits, flowers, leaves and intricate geometric shapes, are as individual as a piece of tapestry and as highly prized as any of the wedding gifts. The most beautiful one I have seen, almost 50 years old, was hanging in pride of place in a living-room on Karpathos. Like the old couple's marriage, it had happily withstood the test of time!

*Left: Blue, blue water meeting the misty hills, boats bobbing in the water and nets drying in the sun – the scene at Hydra. Top: An air of contented tranquility for both shepherd and flock, near Ermioni, Peloponnese. Above: A container garden in a colourful setting near Aegina.*

# SAUSAGE AND PEPPER CASSEROLE

*Spetzofai*

Kalamata, on the Messinian coast and home of the toe-tapping traditional dance, the *kalamatianos*, has an air of familiarity. Typically, the harbour is lined with tavernas, restaurants and rotisseries serving a selection of dishes ranging from fresh fish to – in high season – spit-roast sucking pig.

Just inland, the choice is more homely. We came across a butcher's shop strung from side to side with drying crimson sausages and a blackened pan over a gas flame where some of them were simmering in a hearty sauce. We enjoyed the results on the most splendid of pine tables – a centuries-old butcher's block.

### SERVES 4–6

*750g (1½ lb) dried spiced sausages*
*450g (1lb) red peppers*
*5 tbsp olive oil*
*2 medium onions, thickly sliced*
*225g (8oz) canned tomatoes*
*2 tsp dried oregano*
*salt and black pepper*
*lemon wedges, to serve*

Cut the sausages into 5cm (2in) lengths. Fry them, without any additional fat, in a frying-pan for 5 minutes, turning them with a spoon occasionally. Lift out the sausages, set them aside and discard the fat in the pan.

Halve, core and seed the peppers and cut them into thick chunks.

Heat the oil in a saucepan and fry the onions over medium heat until they are transparent. Add the peppers and continue frying for 2–3 minutes.

Add the tomatoes, oregano and sausages, season with a little salt and plenty of pepper and stir well. Cover the pan and simmer over low heat for 15 minutes until the sausages are coated in a thick, deep red sauce. Taste and adjust the seasoning if necessary – the amount of salt and pepper you need will largely depend on the character of the sausages.

Serve with lemon wedges.

# DOUGHNUTS WITH LEMON SYRUP

*Loukoumades me siropi*

One of the great joys of staying on Poros – apart, that is, from ferry-hopping over to Galata on the mainland and wandering through the romance of lemon groves – is the abundance of doughnut shops sprinkled along the harbour.

After a meal of crisp and crumbling spit-roast lamb, it's quite the thing to while away the rest of the evening with a drink and a dish of light-as-a-feather confections drenched in oh-so-sticky lemon-flavoured syrup.

### MAKES ABOUT 30 DOUGHNUTS

*300ml (½ pint) lukewarm water*
*1 tbsp dried yeast*
*350g (12oz) plain flour*
*1 tsp salt*
*100ml (4fl oz) lukewarm milk*
*2 tbsp honey, melted*
*1 large egg*
*oil, for deep frying*
*1 tsp ground cinnamon*
*lemon wedges, to serve (optional)*

### SYRUP
*225g (8oz) sugar*
*juice of 2 lemons*
*thinly pared strip of lemon rind*
*2–3 tbsp fruit liqueur, such as kumquat liqueur*
*(optional)*

First make the syrup. Put the sugar into a small, heavy-based saucepan and add the lemon juice, lemon rind and 200ml (6fl oz) water. Stir over low heat to dissolve the sugar. Increase the heat and boil rapidly for about 5 minutes until the mixture thickens slightly and becomes sticky enough to coat the back of a spoon. Remove from the heat, discard the lemon rind and stir in the liqueur if used. Pour into a jug and set aside to cool.

To make the doughnuts, pour 3 tbsp of the lukewarm water into a cup or small bowl, sprinkle on the yeast and stir well. Set aside in a warm place for 10 minutes, until the yeast 'works' and the mixture becomes frothy.

Sift the flour and salt into a bowl, make a well in the centre and pour on the yeast mixture, the remaining lukewarm water and the milk and add the honey and egg. Stir to mix the liquids together and then gradually draw the flour into the centre. When it is all incorporated, beat well to form a smooth batter.

Cover the bowl and set aside in a warm place (such as the airing cupboard) for 1 hour until the batter has doubled in volume.

Heat the oil for deep frying. Drop in tablespoons of the mixture and fry them for 3–4 minutes, turning them once, until they are puffed up and golden brown. Toss them on kitchen paper to dry and keep them warm while you cook the rest.

Pile the doughnuts on a warm plate, sprinkle them with cinnamon and serve with the syrup and, if you like, lemon wedges.

---

# APRICOT DESSERT

*Verikoko glyko*

Field upon field of headily scented blossom; men and women working in the orchards and fruit groves from misty morning until dusky night; noisy three-wheelers, shunting boxes of fruit back and forth across the narrow lanes; and rickety roadside stalls piled high with temptingly cheap oranges, lemons, apricots and grapes – whenever you visit the Argolic plain in the eastern Peloponnese, it is a hive of fruitful activity.

This simple recipe for oozingly ripe apricots was served to us on a farm practically in the shadow of ancient Tiryns.

### SERVES 4–6

*1·5kg (3¹/₂ lb) ripe apricots*
*50g (2oz) sugar*
*75g (3oz) split blanched almonds*
*300ml (¹/₂ pint) double cream, stiffly whipped*

Halve, stone and then quarter the apricots. Put half of them in a saucepan with the sugar and 2 tbsp water. Bring them slowly to the boil, stirring to dissolve the sugar and to prevent them from sticking. Cook for 15 minutes or until the fruit collapses. Blend in a liquidizer to make a stiff purée. Fold the remaining quartered apricots and two-thirds of the almonds into the purée. Cool and then chill in the refrigerator.

Arrange layers of the apricot mixture and the cream in a glass bowl or in individual dishes, finishing with cream. Sprinkle the reserved almonds on top and serve chilled. Finger biscuits make a pleasant accompaniment.

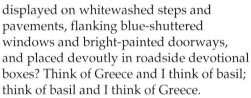

# Basil

How many pots, tubs and painted tins of bushy, bright-leaved basil are there, I wonder, displayed on whitewashed steps and pavements, flanking blue-shuttered windows and bright-painted doorways, and placed devoutly in roadside devotional boxes? Think of Greece and I think of basil; think of basil and I think of Greece.

The plant, which grows as an annual, is thought to be a native of the Middle East , southern Asia and Africa, and it was grown by the ancient Greeks as a culinary and medicinal herb. The variety most favoured in Greece has minute, bright green leaves and a pungent aroma, and it bears white, insignificant flowers throughout the summer.

The slightly spicy leaves have a special affinity with tomatoes, mushrooms and eggs and with poultry dishes, although few Hellenic cooks use the herb to its full potential. In self-help medicine it has been used in the treatment of stomach disorders and sickness, as a mild sedative and as an antiseptic.

In Greece the herb has a special religious significance. Men wear sprigs of the bright green leaves tucked into their hatbands when they go to church on Stavros Day (the Day of the Cross) on 14 September. And a sprig cut from a plant and offered to a visitor is a sign of welcome and friendship.

# CHAPTER 2

# The Cyclades

Picnicking on prickly pears and goats' cheese in the tropical shade of the Valley of the Butterflies, a zoologists' paradise on Paros; coming across a stone-built hut on Milos, as remote as any shepherd's refuge and hung with dark red ribbons of smoke-dried and spicy sausages; buying fruit and vegetables, fresh every day, from donkey panniers driven in from the hillside farms on Mikonos; sitting under the cloudy blue haze of morning glory on Naxos and sipping the sweet golden citron liqueur, tangy with all the aroma and flavour that lemons can yield, and hearing yet once more that it was Dionysos, the god of wine, who taught the islanders the demanding skills of the vintner; jostling precariously in a tossing boat as it chugged away from Folegandros with a commendable bag of game birds destined for the bright restaurants in the cities; getting into the tireless and day-long rhythm of picking olives on Tinos, renowned for the intensity of its religious festivals and the splendour of its processions – the Cyclades, a hoop of some twenty islands rising from the Aegean, supply a feast of food-oriented images, and, indeed, a feast of local dishes that bring together the twin harvest of the sea and the countryside.

From Kea in the north to Anafi in the south, from Andimilos in the west to Amorgos in the east, each island has its proud culinary heritage, artfully concealed, in some cases, behind the uniform façades of trendy tavernas in popular tourist resorts.

Take Andros, for example, with its dazzling, white-washed houses, precipitous pathways and

rugged courtyards. You don't have to wander far from the holiday-making crowd to come across a little place that serves – should you wish it – an aperitif consisting mainly, it seems, of tarragon-flavoured oil and vinegar that tastes like wine, and

*Opposite: The cubist architecture that typifies so many of the Cycladic islands, seen here between Apollonia and Kastron, on Siphnos. Below: The baker, his oven fire raging in the shop behind him, with a tray of dough for sesame-topped bread rings.*

a plate of crisply fried fish served – bliss! – with black figs and rosemary bread.

A visit to a nunnery can be rewarding in more ways than one. I shall be eternally grateful to the island nuns who shared their lunch with us – a dish of baked marrow stuffed simply with the cream and green marbled mixture of rice and eau-de-cologne mint that has been a family favourite ever since. It was there that I first saw the intimate glow created by dried verbascum flowers floating in a lamp of olive oil, a timeless way of lighting that seems to come straight from the heart.

And then there are long country walks. Miles from anywhere, I got chatting to a family working in the fields. The young son shook down a hail of ripe cherries, the daughter spread out her pinny as a tablecloth, and we sat down to a convivial glass of *raki* and a slice of home-made cheese. My offer to make up for lost time was eventually accepted – my one and only experience of scything vetch – until the very last stem was felled. When, at last, the day's work was done, the head of the household piped the workforce off the field with the most haunting music played on a flute cut, on the spot, from an oleander twig. And home to another memorable Cycladic meal.

---

## SPLIT PEA PURÉE

### Fava

I left my own modest monument on Santorini, or Thira, that most romantic of islands with what must be the most awe-inspiring and photogenic roof-line in the Aegean. I helped to lay a sizeable piece of paving, an intricate geometric pattern of grey and white stones that seemed to regroup, like a kaleidoscope, with each change in the direction or intensity of the sunlight.

As a reward, I was invited to share the workman's lunch, right there on the square. We ate it out of yoghurt pots and scooped it up with bread. A similar dish is served in celebration of the island's festival in July.

### SERVES 6

*450g (1lb) yellow split peas, washed and drained*
*1 bay leaf*
*2 medium onions, chopped*
*salt and black pepper*
*3 tbsp olive oil, plus extra to garnish*
*2 tbsp chopped parsley*
*lemon wedges, to serve*
*2 small onions, thinly sliced into rings, to*
*garnish (optional)*

Put the peas and the bay leaf into a large saucepan with 1 litre (1¾ pints) water. Bring to the boil and skim off any foam that rises to the surface. Add the onion, cover the pan and simmer for 1½ hours, stirring occasionally, until the peas have collapsed, absorbed the water and formed a coarse purée. Discard the bay leaf and beat the purée with a wooden spoon. Season with salt and pepper. Beat in the oil.

Turn the purée into a warm serving dish. Drizzle on oil to garnish, and sprinkle with the parsley. Serve warm, with lemon wedges and with piquant onion rings for a sharp flavour contrast, if you wish.

## FISH SOUP

### Kakavia

Fishermen will tell you that there's only one time and place to eat *kakavia*, the fish soup named after the traditional earthenware pot in which it has, for centuries, been cooked – and that's on a fishing boat, miles out to sea, when the fishermen toss in all those fish that are too small or are too insignificant to sell.

The closest I have come to that experience was a ladleful of soup offered to me and the local priest by a fisherman heating up his *kakavi* on the quayside at Naoussa on Paros. The greater the variety of fish you can muster, the closer your soup will be to the fishermen's tradition.

SERVES 6

*1·5kg (3½ lb) mixed fish, such as red mullet,*
*whiting, sea bream*
*1kg (2¼lb) fish trimmings from the fishmonger*
*(optional, see method)*
*2 litres (3½ pints) water or fish stock (see method)*
*150ml (¼ pint) olive oil*
*2 medium onions, sliced*
*2 medium carrots, sliced*
*4 stalks celery, sliced*
*150ml (¼ pint) white wine*
*4 large tomatoes, skinned and sliced*
*450g (1lb) large potatoes, quartered lengthways*
*2 bay leaves*
*a handful of parsley stalks, tied into a bunch*
*juice of 2 lemons*
*salt and black pepper*
*450g (1lb) shelled shrimps or prawns*
*2 tbsp chopped parsley*
*lemon wedges, to serve*

Clean and wash the fish. Small fish can be left whole, or you can remove the heads and tails and fillet them. Prepare larger fish in this way and cut them into slices. You can use the fish trimmings, and more bits, which you can buy from the fishmonger, to make fish stock with extra flavouring vegetables (see page 17). Or, as they do on the fishing boats, you can simply make the soup with water.

Heat the oil in a large pan and fry the onion, carrot and celery over medium heat for 4–5 minutes. Pour on the water or stock and the wine and add the tomatoes, potatoes and bay leaves. Bring to the boil and simmer for 10 minutes.

Add the bunch of parsley, the lemon juice and the larger or firmer types of fish, and cook for 10 minutes. Add smaller fish or fish slices, season with salt and pepper and continue cooking for 5 minutes. Add the shrimps or prawns and cook, without boiling, for 5 minutes. Check that each type of fish is now just tender.

Remove the bunch of parsley. Taste the soup and adjust the seasoning if necessary. It may need a little more lemon juice to sharpen it. Sprinkle with the chopped parsley and serve with lemon wedges.

If whole fish such as red mullet are included in the soup, serve these separately on a plate with the potatoes. The bones are far easier to cope with that way.

## 'Clean Monday'

*Kathari Deftera*, which literally means 'Clean Monday', is the first day of Lent and one of the most notable events in the Greek Orthodox calendar, and, as such, it is an occasion for whole families to take to the countryside for a day of celebration.

The culinary speciality of the day is *lagana*, a flat, unleavened bread thickly covered with sesame seeds. And so the first task of the morning is to join the throng – it's never a queue! – at the baker's to ensure enough supplies to satisfy all those hungry open-air appetites.

As the day marks the beginning of the long Lenten fast, during which meat, eggs and dairy products are prohibited, every family picnic will be a masterpiece of ingenuity, mainly vegetarian style. Luckily, though, for the sake of variety, shellfish and seafood are allowed, and so the main dishes will centre around these versatile ingredients. There might be boiled or pickled octopus with a lemony dressing, squid in tomato sauce, boiled shrimps with chick-peas or dried beans, or, best of all, huge prawns grilled on an open fire.

And then, after the picnic, comes the children's traditional ritual, the launching of the *Kathari Deftera* kites. For weeks before the day families will have been designing and devising colourful and imaginative, realistic and symbolic shapes that will weave and climb ever higher, in keeping with a tradition that, people believe, will help to safeguard the well-being of the family for the year ahead.

And all the while, as the wine is passed around and the glasses clink, the toast is to a good Lent and a happy Easter, *Kali Saracosti kai kalo Pascha.*

# COURGETTE FLOWER FRITTERS

*Tiganita anthi kolokithias*

It was late in the afternoon. We had meandered for miles along flower-fringed lanes, beside gurgling streams and through mellow orchards when we came across a taverna. It was closed. Hearing our voices, the owner insisted on carrying a table, chairs and a bottle of wine into the lane, and disappeared with a reassuring 'leave it to me'.

Some time later he re-emerged with a plate of crispy, golden puffed-up fritters. 'If you are tired,' he said, 'why don't you ride my donkeys down to the bus. No problem. They know their way back.' That's Andros for you.

### SERVES 4

*12 courgette flowers (see method)*
*oil, for deep frying*
*lemon wedges, to serve*

### BATTER
*100g (4oz) plain flour*
*salt*
*3 tbsp olive oil*
*150ml (¼ pint) lukewarm water*
*1 egg white, stiffly whipped*

First make the batter. Sift together the flour and salt and stir in the oil. Gradually beat in the water and mix to a smooth paste. Leave to stand, if possible, for about 1 hour. (I am pleased to say that our man forewent this refinement.) Just before using, fold in the frothy egg white until it is well blended.

If you do not grow courgettes, you may be able to pick some flowers at a pick-your-own farm. Many proprietors who have Middle Eastern customers are well used to selling them and make only a nominal charge.

Open out the courgette flowers, cut off the stamens and any stalk and wash them. Bounce them upside-down on kitchen paper to dry them.

Heat the oil for deep frying. Dip the courgette flowers in the batter – I usually hold them with a pair of tweezers – and allow the excess to drain back into the bowl. Fry the flowers, two or three at a time,

*Pages 30–31: Fish Soup; recipe on page 28.*

turning them once, for about 3 minutes until they are crisp and golden brown. Toss them on kitchen paper to dry them and keep them warm while you fry the remainder.

Serve the fritters with lemon wedges for a first course. To make a meal of them, serve a mixed salad with plenty of feta cheese and rough country bread.

———

# CHEESE PIES

*Tiropittes*

*Tiropittes*, as these melt-in-the-mouth pastries are called, are not, as far as I know, the special preserve of any region of Greece. It's just that the best ones I have ever tasted, tinglingly hot and oozing with their creamy filling, came from the baker's next to the bus-stop high up in Apollonia, the main town of Siphnos. With a treat like that next door, who cares if the bus across the island is a scrap behind schedule or – as occasionally happens – doesn't come at all.

### MAKES ABOUT 10 PIES OR 48 SMALL TRIANGLES

*400g (14oz) packet filo pastry*
*about 75g (3oz) butter, melted*

### FILLING
*25g (1oz) butter*
*4 tsp plain flour*
*4 tbsp milk*
*150ml (¼ pint) single cream*
*175g (6oz) feta cheese, crumbled*
*50g (2oz) graviera or gruyère cheese, grated*
*2 eggs, beaten*
*2 tbsp chopped parsley (flat-leaved variety,*
*if available)*
*black pepper*
*grated nutmeg*

First make the filling. Melt the butter in a small saucepan and stir in the flour. Cook over low heat, stirring all the time, for 1 minute. Gradually pour on the milk and cream, still stirring, and simmer over low heat for 3 minutes. Do not allow the sauce to boil. Set aside to cool.

Stir the cheeses, eggs and parsley into the sauce and season with a few grindings of pepper and a few gratings of nutmeg. Beat until the mixture is well blended.

When using filo pastry, the secret of success is to work quickly before the paper-thin sheet you are shaping has a chance to dry out, and remember to keep the remainder covered with a damp cloth for the same reason.

To make the familiar semicircular pies, which are so much a part of bakers' shops and roadside stalls, cut out circles from the pastry sheets, using a saucer as a guide. Keep out six circles for the first pie and cover the remainder. Brush each circle with butter and stack them one on top of the other. Put the pan over low heat to keep the fat liquid. Place 3 tbsp filling on one side of the pastry circles and fold over to cover it. Press the edges firmly together to seal and brush the top with butter. Continue making more pies in the same way.

Place them on a greased baking sheet and cook them at 180°C (350°F/Gas 4) for 25 minutes until they are golden brown. Serve hot or warm.

To make small bite-sized triangles to serve with drinks, cut one pastry sheet into three strips about 12 x 30cm (5 x 12in). Each strip makes one triangle, so keep the other two strips and the remaining pastry sheets temporarily under wraps.

Brush the pastry strip lightly with melted butter. Fold it in half lengthways and brush it with butter again. Place a teaspoon of the cheese filling close to one end of the pastry, fold the corner over the filling to make a triangle and continue folding all along the length of the strip. Brush the top of the triangle with more butter and place it, join side down, on a greased baking sheet.

Continue making more triangles with the remaining pastry and filling.

Cook the pastries in the oven at 180°C (350°F/Gas 4) for about 20 minutes until they are golden brown and look like fat little cushions. Serve hot, if not straight from the oven then gently reheated.

---

# BAKED OYSTERS

*Streidia sto fourno*

Not all Greek islands are treasure troves of archaeological glories, but Milos has a civilization dating back some 5,000 years – to Minoan times – and excavations to prove it.

There's also a veritable shoal of fishing villages, and each one is completely different from the next.

Ahivadolimni is notable for its beach and prolific oyster beds, but my favourite is Klima, a friendly hotchpotch of rickety-looking houses, where, continuing a timeless custom, the women hold up colourful cloths and form a swaying line along the shore to greet passing ships.

## SERVES 4

*24 oysters*
*175g (6oz) parsley butter (see below)*
*4 tbsp graviera or gruyère cheese, grated*
*4 tbsp dried breadcrumbs*
*lemon wedges, to serve*

### PARSLEY BUTTER
*175g (6oz) unsalted butter, softened*
*1 small onion or shallot, finely chopped*
*2 cloves garlic, crushed*
*2 tsp lemon juice*
*3 tbsp chopped parsley*
*black pepper*

First, make the parsley butter. Beat the butter in a bowl and beat in the onion, garlic, lemon juice and parsley. Season with pepper. Shape into a roll, wrap in foil and chill until needed.

Wash the oysters in a large bowl of water and scrub them thoroughly. Open the shells, using a thick, heavy-bladed knife or a special tool. Strain off the liquor through a piece of fine muslin or cheesecloth to trap any sand and reserve it for another dish. The liquor is pure delight to add to fish soup of any kind, and brings an exotic – though not very Greek – touch to a vodka and tomato juice cocktail.

Remove the oysters and place each one in the deep half-shell. Arrange them in the hollows in two bun tins or on a baking tray spread with a layer of sand or cooking salt. You simply push the shells down to make cavities, until they sit securely. Flake the butter over the oysters. Then mix together the cheese and the breadcrumbs and sprinkle them evenly on top.

Bake the oysters in the oven at 190°C (375°F/Gas 5) for 10 minutes until the topping is golden brown. Serve hot, with the lemon wedges and plenty of rough bread.

## POTATO AND SAUSAGE OMELETTE

*Froutalia*

It seems to me that the greatest privilege on earth is to share a meal with a family which lives, of necessity, on the fruits of its labours – potatoes, dried sausage, eggs, beans, olive oil … whatever there is.

Deep in the agricultural heartland of Andros, a world away from the cafés and beaches, we watched in wonder as Adonis and Maria prepared *froutalia*, a local speciality, in the outdoor kitchen behind their tiny cottage. The dish was, truly, a feast.

### SERVES 4–6

*1kg (2¼lb) potatoes*
*oil, for deep frying, and extra for sprinkling (optional)*
*8 eggs*
*salt and black pepper*
*450g (1lb) dried spicy sausage , cut into small chunks*
*2 tbsp chopped parsley*

Peel the potatoes, cut them into fingers as for chips and dry them on kitchen paper. Heat the oil for deep frying and fry the chips until they are crisp and golden. Lift them out of the oil with a draining spoon and toss them on kitchen paper to dry them. Keep them warm.

Beat the eggs with 3 tbsp water, season with salt and pepper (the amount you use will depend on the character of the sausage) and stir in the sausage.

Place the chips in a large heated frying-pan (Adonis used a round aluminium pan) and pour the egg mixture over them. Cook over high heat for 2–3 minutes, shaking the pan once or twice. Put it under a hot grill for a further 2–3 minutes, until the eggs are set and golden brown on top. Sprinkle with parsley and slice into wedges to serve. Sprinkle the top with olive oil if you wish.

Our *froutalia* was served with green beans, lightly steamed and tossed in olive oil and lemon juice,

*Pages 34–5: Siphnos is notable for having over 300 churches.*

and dried broad beans, cooked and served cold in a fresh tomato sauce. The huge round loaf, made from the family's own flour, was cooked in the outside oven fuelled with rosemary and oleander twigs.

## GOAT AND HARICOT CASSEROLE

*Katsikaki kai fasolia yiouvetsi*

They have wonderful ways of cooking goat on Siphnos. I have been chatting in a farm cottage when the son has come in with a goat-stew take-away from a restaurant down on the harbour, and I have dipped an eager spoon into a dish – this dish – that had been cooked overnight at the baker's and sent home on the bus.

If you can buy goat's meat – perhaps in an Asian butcher's – do, for the flavour is unmistakable, but if you cannot, substitute lamb, cut from the shoulder.

### SERVES 4–6

*450g (1lb) dried haricot beans, soaked overnight and drained*
*3 tbsp olive oil*
*2 medium onions, sliced*
*2 cloves garlic, chopped*
*1kg (2¼lb) lean goat's meat, cubed*
*225g (8oz) canned tomatoes, chopped*
*2 tbsp tomato purée*
*1 stick cinnamon*
*salt and black pepper*
*1 tbsp lemon juice*
*1 tbsp chopped parsley*

Fast-boil the beans in a pan of unsalted water for 10 minutes. Lower the heat and simmer them for a further 30 minutes, then drain them and set aside.

Heat the oil in a flameproof casserole and fry the onions over medium heat until they are transparent. Add the garlic and cook for 1–2 minutes more.

Stir in the meat and turn it over and over with a wooden spoon until it is lightly coloured on all sides. Add the tomatoes, tomato purée and 450ml (¾ pint) water and stir well until the sauce is blended. Add the cinnamon and bring to the boil.

Cover the casserole and cook in the oven at 170°C (325°F/Gas 3) for 2½–2¾ hours until the meat is tender. Remove the cinnamon stick, season well with salt and pepper and stir in the lemon juice. Sprinkle on the parsley to serve.

Often bread is considered accompaniment enough, but I find that boiled potatoes are always welcome.

---

# BRAISED HARE

## *Lagos stifatho*

A hubbub of would-be landladies meets the ferry as it glides into port at Amorgos, even in the black of night. But there was no need to wait until dawn to discover that our room was but a trapdoor away from the winery; two massive barrels of *mavros* wine in its extreme infancy create the headiest and least sleep-provoking aroma around! The deep red and cloudy wine, a cheap and much appreciated local currency, and certainly more plentiful than water, cropped up in meal after meal.

This braised hare, cooked Saturday-night-come-Sunday-morning, was our hostess's special tribute to 'new friends from across the sea'. You need to start a day before serving.

### SERVES 6

*1 hare, about 2kg (4½ lb), jointed*
*300ml (½ pint) malt vinegar*
*8 tbsp plain flour*
*1 tbsp dried oregano*
*black pepper*
*150ml (¼ pint) olive oil*
*2 tbsp tomato purée*
*2 tbsp honey*
*1kg (2¼lb) small onions or shallots*
*2 tbsp chopped parsley*

### MARINADE
*600ml (1 pint) full-bodied red wine*
*2 tbsp red wine vinegar*
*1 medium onion, sliced*
*2 medium carrots, sliced*
*2 stalks celery, sliced*
*1 tbsp salt*
*4 whole cloves*
*6 juniper berries, crushed*
*1 tbsp black peppercorns, crushed*
*4–6 sprigs thyme*
*2–3 stalks parsley*

Wash the hare and put it in a large bowl with the vinegar and enough water to cover. Leave to soak for 1–2 hours, then remove it.

To make the marinade, pour the wine and red wine vinegar into a bowl. Add the onion, carrot, celery and salt. Tie the spices and herbs in a square of muslin and add then to the marinade. Add the hare, pushing each piece into the liquid. Cover and leave in the refrigerator for about 24 hours, turning the hare in the marinade occasionally. Drain and dry the hare. Strain and reserve the marinade liquid. Discard the flavouring vegetables (or use them in soup) and the spices and herbs. Toss the hare in the flour seasoned with the oregano and pepper.

Heat 6 tbsp of the oil in a large flameproof casserole – our hostess had a black iron one that had served the family for generations – and fry the hare, a few pieces at a time, until it is lightly coloured and sealed on all sides.

Lift out the hare and sprinkle any remaining flour into the casserole. Stir in the marinade liquid, the tomato purée and honey and bring to the boil. Add the hare, cover the casserole and cook in the oven at 180°C (350°F/Gas 4) for 2 hours.

Blanch the onions or shallots in boiling water for 2 minutes, then drain them. Heat the remaining oil in a pan and fry them for 4–5 minutes until they begin to colour. Drain them and add them to the casserole. Continue cooking for 1–1½ hours until the hare is tender. Taste the sauce and adjust the seasoning if necessary. If it tastes the slightest bit thin, stir in another 1 tbsp honey. Sprinkle on the parsley before serving.

*Top: Blue, white and gold, the vibrant combination of colours that, in every shape, texture and permutation, characterizes the island of Santorini. Above: Almost everyone is involved at harvest time! A priest winnows corn beneath the sails of a windmill on Paros. Left: Braised Hare; recipe on page 37.*

# HONEY AND CHEESE PIE

### *Kithnopitta*

Time passes lazily by on Kithnos, one of the most northerly of the Cyclades group. It's very relaxing, I find, watching other people work! I had been chatting for some while to an old basketmaker, his nimble fingers in tune with generations of the island's craftsmen, when he produced a slice of a sweet and heavily spiced flan. His wife wasn't on hand to pass on the recipe, so this is my own approximation, with a somewhat lighter touch on the cinnamon.

### SERVES 8

*75g (3oz) unsalted butter, slightly softened*
*75g (3oz) ricotta or curd cheese, sieved*
*125g (5oz) plain flour*
*salt*
*1/2 tsp ground cinnamon*

### FILLING
*450g (1lb) ricotta or curd cheese, sieved*
*4 eggs*
*50g (2oz) ground almonds*
*2 tsp ground cinnamon*
*125g (5oz) honey*

To make the pastry, cream the butter and cheese until the mixture is soft. Sift together the flour, salt and cinnamon and sprinkle on to the cheese mixture. Blend together to form a soft ball and knead lightly. Wrap in foil and chill for about 30 minutes.

Roll out the pastry on a lightly floured board and use it to line a greased and floured 22cm (9in) flan dish. Trim the edges and prick the base many times with a fork. Line the pastry with greaseproof paper, fill it with a layer of dried beans and bake in the oven at 190°C (375°F/Gas 5) for 15 minutes. Remove the paper and beans and leave the pastry case to cool.

To make the filling, beat together the cheese, eggs, ground almonds, 1 tsp of the cinnamon and the honey until the mixture is smooth and well blended.

Pour the mixture into the partly baked pastry case and bake in the oven at the same temperature for 35 minutes until the filling is set and the top a deep golden brown. Sprinkle with the remaining cinnamon.

Serve warm or cold, with single cream or yogurt.

---

# HALVA WITH PISTACHIOS

### *Halvas me fistikia*

Ermoupolis, the main town of Siros, is the capital of the Cycladic province, and, at first sight, it presents an uncompromisingly commercial face – not the stuff that tourist brochures are made of. But only a short bicycle ride away you're into mile after therapeutic mile of vineyards, orchards and melon fields.

Stop at any *kafenion* for refreshment and you'll soon find that the islanders have winning ways with sweetmeats, especially halva, nougat and Turkish delight.

### MAKES ABOUT 750g (1½lb)

*175g (6oz) butter, softened*
*175g (6oz) sugar*
*4 eggs*
*450g (1lb) coarse-grained semolina*
*140g (5½oz) pistachios (or use blanched almonds)*
*1 tsp ground cinnamon*

### SYRUP
*225g (8oz) sugar*
*2 tsp lemon juice*
*1 stick cinnamon*

Beat together the butter and sugar until the mixture is light and creamy. Beat in the eggs one at a time and continue beating until the mixture is smooth and shows no sign of curdling. Beat in the semolina a little at a time, and continue beating until the mixture is smooth again. Stir in the nuts and cinnamon.

Pour the mixture into a greased tin, 18cm (7in) square, and level the top. Bake in the oven at 180°C (350°F/Gas 4) for about 40–45 minutes until the 'cake' is crisp.

Meanwhile, make the syrup. Put the sugar, lemon juice and cinnamon into a heavy-bottomed pan with 450ml (¾ pint) water. Stir over low heat until the sugar has dissolved, then increase the heat, bring to the boil and fast-boil for about 5 minutes until the syrup is sticky and thick enough to coat the back of a spoon. Remove the cinnamon.

As soon as you take the halva from the oven, pour the syrup evenly over the surface. Set aside to cool, when the cake will have absorbed the syrup. Cut into squares and serve as a sweetmeat with coffee and chilled water.

---

# Honey

For me, one of the most memorable of rural sights is a clutch of beehives straddling a gentle hillside, drawing the eye gradually across a flower-speckled meadow or – and this is one of my most treasured memories of Lefkas – clustered busily in a petal-strewn orchard. Painted blue and green and yellow, sometimes striped and usually sun-bleached, the square wooden hives are as familiar a part of the island scene as are jars of clear and set honey – take your choice – on the grocers' shelves.

Every island and almost every region has its own speciality, sometimes sold proudly in unlabelled jars, sometimes, more formally, in blue and white cans. Look or ask for the magic word *meli*, and take stock of the local agricultural, horticultural and botanical scene: the bees do!

Some Greek honeys have a unique, almost nutty flavour. Some smell and taste deliciously of wild thyme flowers, some of citrus blossom. Others, which have a powerful scent, emanate from orchards of chestnut blossom.

These regional honeys give their distinctive flavours to oh-so-gooey pastries, such as *baklava* and *kataifi*, and sometimes to the syrup served with doughnuts. But for me, the essence of enjoyment is when the honey is drizzled, golden, glowing and temptingly aromatic, over my breakfast yoghurt.

---

# RICE PUDDING

*Rizogalo*

Island-hoppers know Anafi as the next ferry stop after Santorini, charting a sometimes choppy course due east. Mythology buffs know that, according to legend, the island wouldn't have existed at all if it weren't for the Argonauts. It is said to have risen from the sea at Apollo's command to give them shelter from a storm.

The island is at its brightest in the autumn, when the annual festival of songs and dances takes place. This rice pudding, or one very like it, is always part of the celebrations.

### SERVES 6

*100g (4oz) short-grain rice, washed and drained*
*salt*
*600ml (1 pint) milk*
*600ml (1 pint) single cream*
*2 tsp cornflour*
*2 egg yolks*
*50g (2oz) vanilla sugar (see method)*
*1 tsp vanilla essence*
*grated nutmeg*

Put the rice into a saucepan with 300ml (½ pint) water. Bring to the boil and simmer, uncovered, over low heat, stirring occasionally, until the rice has absorbed the water, which takes about 10 minutes.

Add the salt, milk and cream, bring to simmering point and simmer, uncovered, for about 15 minutes until the rice is very tender. Stir the rice occasionally during this time.

Blend the cornflour to a smooth paste with 2 tbsp water, beat in the egg yolks and add to the rice in the pan. Stir in the sugar (if you have some that has been stored in a jar with a vanilla pod, so much the better) and vanilla essence, and stir over low heat until the rice is thick and creamy. Make sure you do not allow it to boil.

Turn the rice out into a serving bowl or – as the Greeks do – when it has cooled slightly, into individual glass dishes and dust the top with a few gratings of nutmeg. Serve warm or cold.

# CHAPTER 3

# The Dodecanese

The Dodecanese, the 'twelve islands' (fourteen, actually), which emerge rockily from the shadow of the Turkish coastline, are an island-hopper's paradise. Armed with a ferry-boat timetable which, although not always accurate, is at least a guide – you can plan to leapfrog from one to another, lunching here, dining there, and enjoying a real taste of island individuality.

Strangely enough, some of my own most vivid gastronomic memories of Dodekanisa seem to centre around transport, ferry-boat or otherwise. There was the long, long haul from Piraeus to Rhodes, when I first became addicted to cheese pies (the only food, apart from toast, on sale at the bar – luckily they were good ones) and to a certain tantalizing and haunting folk song of, inevitably, unrequited love.

It was on Rhodes, too, when we had miraculously cracked the mysteries of the bus timetable and struck across country in a way the compilers had never envisaged, that we had the most surprising meal. Surprising in that it was served at a taverna on a noisy, busy, traffic-jammed crossroads, a background that faded into tranquil obscurity as we appreciated first a spicy fish and vegetable soup, then cold globe artichokes brimming over with prawns, and then a salad of fried aubergines and peppers. It was a stroke of luck, incidentally, that I overheard the bus driver telling a crony that he would be returning an hour earlier than scheduled so that he could take his wife to the dentist. It would have been a long and dusty trek back to base!

On Karpathos it was nearly a case of no transport at all to take us over, round or through the Profitis Ilias mountain to reach the remote north of the island, where the women wear magnificently embroidered and jewelled costumes and villagers speak a challenging mixture of Greek and Doric dialect. It isn't easy to get from Pigathia to Diafani and Olimbos when the sea is too rough for the ferry to sail round the island, when the caique owner is on his honeymoon and when the most reliable four-

*Opposite: High-rise living around the bay of Karpathos.*
*Below: Rhodes is the island for doorways; carved and moulded examples spanning the centuries, line every street.*

wheel drive vehicle is in dock. Perhaps it was the eventual sense of achievement that made roast lamb stuffed with quinces (see page 48) seem like food for the gods.

On Cos, a short ferry-hop from Kalymnos to the north and Nissyros to the south, our bicycles became the key to a meal to remember. Two of us collided, handlebars firmly locked, as we wheeled around to marvel at the red-gold-purple of the sunset over the misty hills. Hearing the commotion, an elderly man – we christened him Uncle Ouzo – came out of a pomegranate grove and invited us into his cottage garden. Now it just so happened – as things do – that he had a shoal of gigantic prawns sizzling on the barbecue; the best possible cure, he insisted, for grazed knees and hurt pride. And he was right. Why we decided to call him Uncle Ouzo is another story.

---

## BAKED CRAB

### *Kavouras sto fourno*

In ancient times Astypalea, the hour-glass shaped island on the west of the Dodecanese group, was known as Ichthyoessa, or island of the fish. And in the bartering that forms the ebb and flow of commercial life on the quaysides and the sea-fresh fare on offer in the modest tavernas that serve the fishing villages, that description is equally apt today.

We were lucky enough to come across a dish that, although not exactly an island speciality, is served on highdays and holidays by a delightful seaside landlady.

### SERVES 6

*2 boiled crabs, about 1kg (2½ lb) each*
*salt and black pepper*
*40g (1½ oz) butter*
*100g (4oz) mushrooms, thinly sliced*
*8 tbsp red wine*
*2 tbsp chopped parsley*
*4 tbsp double cream*
*2 eggs*
*300ml (½ pint) Greek yoghurt*
*nutmeg*
*50g (2oz) graviera or gruyère cheese, grated*

To prepare each crab, place it on its back and twist off the legs and claws. Remove and discard the pointed flap. Take out the main body part, the bone, the meat and the harmful dead man's fingers, which you must discard. Crack the legs and claws and scrape out the meat from these and the body crevices. Mix it well with the rest of the meat, season with salt and pepper and set aside.

Melt the butter in a small saucepan and fry the mushrooms over medium heat for 3–4 minutes until they have absorbed the fat. Pour on the wine, bring to the boil and cook for 3–4 minutes until most of the liquid has evaporated. Remove from the heat, stir in the parsley and cream and season with salt and pepper. Divide the mixture among six shallow ovenproof dishes – or you could use large scallop shells – then add the crab meat, spreading it over the mushrooms.

Beat the eggs into the yoghurt, season with salt and pepper and a few gratings of nutmeg and spoon the sauce over the crab. Sprinkle on the grated cheese.

Bake in oven at 190°C (375°F/Gas 5) for about 15 minutes until the sauce is set and the cheese bubbling and brown. Serve hot.

## PRAWNS IN WINE SAUCE

### *Garithes krasates*

I'm normally totally relaxed about the casual attitude one encounters in many Greek restaurants. After all, sitting there, bemused by the slap-slapping of the waves against the harbour, and with a bottle of retsina on the table, who's in a hurry? But on Symi we were. The boat back to Rhodes was signalling imminent departure, and we had only just been served.

So here is a dish I remember for its inelegance – we scooped it up, sauce and all, into paper napkins, left the requisite number of drachs and just made it aboard.

SERVES 4

50g (2oz) butter
1 medium onion, chopped
1 clove garlic, finely chopped
225g (8oz) canned tomatoes, chopped
2–3 sprigs thyme
5cm (2in) piece cinnamon
100ml (4fl oz) white wine
salt and black pepper
750g (1½ lb) prawns, shelled
5 tbsp double cream
1 tbsp chopped parsley

Melt the butter in a pan and fry the onion over medium heat until it is transparent. Add the garlic and fry for 1–2 minutes more. Stir in the tomatoes, add the thyme, cinnamon and wine and season with salt and pepper.

Bring the sauce to the boil and simmer, uncovered, for 20 minutes until it is reduced to a thick paste. Discard the thyme sprigs. You may, if you like a smooth paste, liquidize it in a blender or food processor at this stage. If so, return the sauce to the cleaned pan, add the prawns and heat through. Stir in the cream and heat gently. Taste the sauce and adjust the seasoning if necessary. Sprinkle parsley to serve.

Boiled rice is a good accompaniment.

———————

# TUNA WITH GARLIC SAUCE

*Tonnos me skorthalia*

One of our visits to Rhodes coincided, in early September, with the start of the tuna-fishing season, and it seemed to us that taverna owners all around the harbour were vying with each other to serve this most succulent of fish, fried, baked, grilled, with sauce, without sauce, every whichway.

A friend who was with us tried this garlic sauce – *skorthalia* – for the first time, and thereafter asked for it to be served with potatoes, beans, steak, chops, chicken and even to heap on plain bread.

SERVES 4

4 tbsp plain flour
salt and black pepper
1 tbsp dried oregano
4 tuna steaks, 175–200g (6–7oz) each, washed
and dried
oil, for shallow frying
lemon wedges, to serve

SAUCE
4 thick slices day-old bread, crusts removed
6 cloves garlic, sliced
3 tbsp lemon juice
150ml (¼ pint) olive oil
salt and black pepper
2 tbsp chopped parsley (optional)

First make the sauce. Crumble the bread in a bowl and cover it with water. Leave it to soak for 15–20 minutes. Tip it into a sieve and press out the excess moisture.

Blend the bread, garlic and lemon juice in a liquidizer or food processor until it is smooth. Then pour in the oil a teaspoon or so at a time, blending to incorporate it all the while. (It's a bit like making mayonnaise, but rather less critical.)

Turn the sauce into a bowl, season with salt and pepper and stir in the parsley if you use it. Cover and set aside for at least 1 hour for the flavours to blend and mellow.

Season the flour with salt, pepper and the oregano and toss the fish steaks in it to coat them thoroughly.

Heat oil for shallow frying in a large, heavy-bottomed frying-pan, and fry the tuna steaks for 4–5 minutes on each side, depending on thickness, until the fish is just firm.

Serve the fish with lemon wedges and offer the sauce separately.

Sadly, these days, even the most orthodox of Greek cooks are inclined to serve chips with this basic island fare, but you could go against the trend and offer plain boiled potatoes instead. To my mind, they are infinitely better suited to the rich, creamy sauce.

## MUSSEL PILAFF

*Mithia pilafi*

The brave men of Kalymnos are not just fishermen – they are sponge fishermen. If you should be there in spring when the fleet sets off for its long and hazardous journey to the shores of Egypt and Libya, be prepared to get caught up in much weeping and wailing and, if you're lucky, in the traditional family Dinner of Love.

We were enjoying a quiet plate of mussels at a waterside taverna when we got involved in a family celebration of a different kind, when an entire wedding party came *sirtaki*-ing along the beach. It's true what they say: the Greeks really do know how to enjoy themselves.

### SERVES 4

*5 tbsp olive oil*
*2 medium onions, finely chopped*
*1kg (2lb) mussels, scrubbed and washed*
*150ml (¼ pint) white wine*
*225g (8oz) long-grain rice, washed and drained*
*salt and black pepper*
*5 tbsp double cream*
*2 tbsp chopped parsley*
*lemon wedges, to serve*

Heat the oil in a large pan and fry the onion over medium heat until it is transparent. Add the mussels and stir them around until they begin to open. Pour on the wine and 450ml (¾ pint) water and bring to the boil. Cover the pan and simmer for 10 minutes. Remove from the heat and lift out the mussels with a draining spoon. Ruthlessly discard any that have not opened.

Add the rice to the pan, season with salt and pepper, stir well and cook for 10–15 minutes, until it is almost tender. If it dries out in the cooking, add a little more water.

Meanwhile, remove the mussels from their shells and discard the shells. Return the mussels to the pan, stir in the cream and adjust the seasoning if necessary. Allow to heat through gently. Sprinkle with parsley and serve with lemon wedges.

Serve with a tomato salad drizzled with oil and covered with a generous layer of purple onion rings.

*Left: Mussel Pilaff.*

## ROAST LAMB WITH QUINCES

*Arni psito me kythonia*

Part-way between Rhodes and Crete, Karpathos enjoys a relative obscurity long since denied its more highly favoured neighbours. With its greenest of green valleys and fertile plains like intricately woven agricultural tapestries, the island is noted for the variety and quality of its fruit.

There comes a time, late in the autumn, when huge golden quinces shine like fairy lights on the leafless trees. That's the time when the islanders make this traditional Sunday dish.

### SERVES 6

*1 leg of lamb, about 2kg (4½ lb), boned*
*2 tbsp lemon juice*
*2 tbsp olive oil*
*salt and black pepper*
*1 tbsp dried oregano*
*lemon wedges, to serve*

#### STUFFING
*3 tbsp olive oil*
*1 medium onion, chopped*
*25g (1oz) butter*
*225g (8oz) ripe quinces, peeled and chopped*
*(or use apples)*
*50g (2oz) long-grain rice, washed and drained*
*50g (2oz) blanched almonds, chopped*
*1 tsp cumin seeds, crushed*
*200ml (6fl oz) cloudy apple juice or water*
*3 tbsp chopped parsley*
*2 tbsp lemon juice*
*salt and black pepper*

First, make the stuffing. Heat the oil in a frying-pan and fry the onion over medium heat until it is transparent. Add the butter and, when it has melted, add the quince and rice and stir well.

Cook for 2 minutes, then add the almonds and cumin seeds and pour on the apple juice or water. Stir well, bring to the boil, cover the pan and simmer for about 8 minutes until the rice is beginning to soften and has absorbed most of the liquid. Remove the pan from the heat, stir in the parsley and lemon juice; season with salt and pepper. Set aside to cool.

Pack the filling into the cavity in the lamb and sew up the meat to make a neat shape. Rub the meat on all sides with the lemon juice and olive oil, season it well with salt and pepper and rub in the oregano.

Place the lamb in a roasting tin and cook in the oven at 220°C (425°F/Gas 7) for 15 minutes. Reduce the heat to 190°C (375°F/Gas 5) and continue cooking for 1½–1¾ hours, turning the meat once, until the meat is as 'pink' or as well done as you like it. (The Greeks tend to enjoy their lamb in a way that many cooks consider overdone.)

Allow the lamb to stand for 15 minutes before carving. Serve with lemon wedges.

---

## LAMB WITH LETTUCE

*Arni me maroulia*

We were studying a map of the ancient site of the Asklepion, the fourth-century BC infirmary and medical school close to the town of Cos, when a helpful young local student broke into our reverie in the broadest of American accents: 'You know about Hippocrates? Him very clever guy.' So that's what the great man of medicine will be, in our family, for ever more!

This delicious springtime recipe introduces the crisp and compact lettuces that take their name from the island on which they originated.

### SERVES 4

*4 tbsp olive oil*
*1kg (2¼lb) lamb, cut from the shoulder and cubed*
*2 medium onions, sliced*
*2 young leeks, white part only, thinly sliced*
*450ml (¾ pint) hot water (or use chicken stock)*
*150ml (¼ pint) white wine*
*salt and black pepper*
*4 tbsp chopped dill or 1 tbsp dried dill weed*
*1 small Cos lettuce, outer leaves removed, and cut*
*into 8 wedges*
*3 eggs*
*juice of 2 lemons*
*2 tbsp chopped parsley*

Heat the oil in a large saucepan and fry half the meat over medium heat, stirring it often, until it is lightly coloured on all sides. Lift it out with a draining spoon and fry the remainder of the meat in the same way. Remove the second batch of meat.

Fry the onion in the fat in the pan for 2–3 minutes, stirring once or twice. Add the leeks and fry for a further 3 minutes.

Return the meat to the pan, pour on the water or stock and the wine, season with salt and pepper and add the dill. Stir well, bring to the boil, cover and simmer for about 1 hour.

Add the lettuce wedges and cook for a further 15 minutes until they are just beginning to soften – they should still have a 'bite' to them.

Beat the eggs with the lemon juice and beat in 2 tbsp water. Spoon in 5–6 tbsp of the sauce from the pan, then pour the egg mixture over the lamb. Stir to blend it well and cook over low heat for 2–3 minutes, until the sauce has heated through, but the eggs have not had a chance to curdle. Sprinkle with parsley to serve.

Boiled pasta, tossed in butter and chopped parsley, goes particularly well with this dish.

## Olives

Whoever it was who first picked a wild olive from a tree and ate it might well have stifled the trade in preserved olives before it ever began. For it takes a quantum leap of the imagination to believe that the bitter, acrid flavour of the raw, untreated fruit can be neutralized just by soaking in brine. How lucky for us that it can!

The offending natural ingredient is a bitter alkaloid that is drawn out when the olives are soaked in a strong alkaline solution or, as green ones often are, layered with rock salt.

As the barrels, drums and sacks of olives so temptingly displayed in the large food markets reveal, it is not just a question of choosing black, sun-ripened fruits or green ones, which are picked before they ripen. No, it is much more fun than that. Olives vary considerably in size, shape, colour and flavour, and retailers won't mind at all if you ask to taste the various types before making your choice.

The ripe olives harvested on Corfu, which are picked up from all those miles and miles of black netting that cover the island, are jet black and glistening, and specially recommended for use in salads. Those cultivated in the Sporades group of islands are rounder and more fleshy, and the ones from Samos, called *throumbes*, are copper-coloured and somewhat shrivelled. Those from Thassos have, perhaps, the most 'bitter-olive' flavour of all, while those from Kalamata in the Peloponnese – a variety

also cultivated on Crete – are much sweeter. These Kalamata olives, which, happily, find their way into my local delicatessen, are ideal for garnishing. I find that their shimmering blue and purple and mauve and brown colours tone to perfection with a flourish of purple sage leaves.

When you buy olives 'loose', or indeed if you buy them packaged or bottled in brine, rinse them in clear water, pack them tightly into jars and cover them with olive oil. Add a few coriander seeds, a clove or two of garlic, a few sprigs of thyme or some bay leaves, what you will. Close the jars and store them in a cool, dark place but not in the refrigerator. When you have served the olives, the oil will have a pungent and very 'Greek' flavour, which is good in salad dressings and all kinds of cooking.

And as for the olives themselves – well, you will need a generous supply if you are to serve them, heaped high in a bowl, with ouzo, in Greek country salad, in a casserole with chicken, in a stuffing for chicken and other poultry, in a delicious savoury bread, as a refreshing snack with thick chunks of bread and a glass of retsina or as a garnish for almost any savoury dish you care to mention.

# CHICKEN WITH OLIVES

*Kotopoulo me elies*

It's like turning back the clock, setting out from the cosmopolitan bustle of Cos town up into the Dikeos mountain region to explore the Asfendiou group of villages.

A small child rushes out to beg a ride on one's bicycle, his mother counters with the gift of sugared almonds, and a neighbour breaks off the corner of a loaf, crisply baked in an outdoor oven and smelling, deliciously, of rosemary branches. And into that same beehive oven goes a casserole heavy with spices and piquant with juicy black olives. Something like this.

### SERVES 4

*4 chicken joints, dried*
*salt and black pepper*
*25g (1oz) butter*
*4 tbsp olive oil*
*2 medium onions, sliced*
*200ml (6fl oz) white wine*
*1 stick cinnamon*
*2 tsp fennel seed, lightly crushed*
*1 tsp cumin seed*
*1 tsp cornflour*
*about 24 large black olives*
*1 tbsp lemon juice*
*2 tbsp chopped parsley*

Season the chicken on all sides with salt and pepper. Heat the butter and oil in a large frying-pan and fry the chicken pieces over medium heat until they are light golden brown. Remove the chicken and set it aside.

Fry the onion in the pan until it is transparent, then return the chicken to the pan. Pour on the wine and add the cinnamon stick. Tie the spice seeds in a piece of muslin and add these to the pan. Spoon the sauce over the chicken.

Bring the sauce to the boil, cover the pan and simmer very slowly for 35–40 minutes until the chicken is nearly tender.

Remove the cinnamon and spice seeds. Mix the cornflour to a smooth paste with 2 tbsp water and stir it into the sauce. Add the olives and lemon juice – which enhances their flavour – and continue cooking for 10–15 minutes until the chicken is well cooked. To test it, insert a skewer into the thick part of the leg. Any juices that spurt out should be clear, not pink. Taste the sauce and adjust the seasoning if necessary.

Arrange the chicken on a heated serving dish and sprinkle the parsley over it.

Buttered noodles or boiled rice make good accompaniments.

*Top: A bell tower, rounded domes and tall masts comprise the harbourside perspective on Kalymnos. Below: Tending an outdoor oven on Karpathos. Right: Chicken with Olives.*

## VEAL RAGOUT

*Mosharaki stifatho*

There seems to be a special quality to the sunlight on Patmos, a certain radiance, a golden glow that softens the formidable outlines of the imposing eleventh-century Monastery of St John the Divine and paints with burnt umber the terraced fields that rise towards it.

We stayed in the shadow of the Monastery – most of the old town of Hora is, to be honest – and came back every day to a homely casserole. Sometimes lamb, sometimes baby goat, sometimes, as here, tender, lemon-flavoured veal.

### SERVES 4

6 tbsp olive oil
1kg (2¼lb) stewing veal, cubed
450g (1lb) small onions or shallots
4 cloves garlic, finely chopped
4 large tomatoes, peeled and chopped
2 bay leaves
1 tsp dried thyme
1 stick cinnamon
150ml (¼ pint) white wine
2 tbsp lemon juice
450ml (¾ pint) light chicken stock or water
salt and black pepper

Heat the oil in a saucepan and fry the veal in two batches over medium heat, stirring so that it browns evenly on all sides. Lift out with a draining spoon and set it aside.

Fry the onions in the oil for 4–5 minutes until they just begin to colour. Add the garlic and fry for 1 minute more. Return the meat to the pan, add the tomatoes, bay leaves, thyme and cinnamon, then pour on the wine, lemon juice and stock or water and season with salt and pepper. Stir well, bring slowly to the boil, cover the pan and simmer for 1½–1¾ hours, stirring from time to time, until the meat is tender. Add a little more stock or water if the sauce dries out.

Taste the sauce and adjust the seasoning if necessary. Finally, remove the bay leaves and cinnamon stick.

Serve with plain boiled potatoes and lightly cooked spinach or, in Greece, wild greens, tossed in olive oil and lemon juice.

## PARTRIDGE WITH SPAGHETTI

*Perthikes me spageto*

Nissyros is an island of dramatic contrasts. It is dominated by the massive but by-now inactive volcano that rises up to an awesome peak in the centre, and is characterized by sparkling white houses that might have been carved out of thick, thick sugar icing.

I remember the island with particular affection for a certain taverna owner who served us with a plate of 'only spaghetti' when – and a nod's as good as a wink in any language – the partridge hidden beneath it was not yet in season.

### SERVES 4

2 large oven-ready partridges, washed and dried
2 tbsp lemon juice
salt and black pepper
50g (2oz) butter
3 tbsp olive oil
350g (12oz) spaghetti
2 tbsp chopped parsley

### SAUCE

3 tbsp olive oil
2 medium onions, sliced
2 cloves garlic, chopped
2 stalks celery, thinly sliced
2 medium carrots, diced
450g (1lb) canned tomatoes, chopped
100ml (4fl oz) red wine
2 tsp sugar
2 bay leaves
1 tbsp dried oregano
salt and black pepper

Sprinkle the birds with lemon juice and season them well with salt and pepper. Heat the butter and oil in a roasting pan, place the birds in the pan, baste them well with the oil and roast in the oven at 180°C (350°/Gas 4) for 45–50 minutes, basting them occasionally.

Meanwhile, make the sauce. Heat the oil in a saucepan and fry the onion over medium heat until it is transparent. Add the garlic, celery and carrot and fry for 2–3 minutes, stirring once or twice. Add the tomatoes, wine, sugar, bay leaves and oregano, season with salt and pepper and bring the sauce to the boil. Simmer, uncovered, for 30–35 minutes, stirring occasionally. Discard the bay leaves.

Cook the spaghetti in a large pan of boiling, salted water for 10–12 minutes or according to the directions on the packet. Drain it in a colander, refresh it by running hot water through it and drain well.

Toss the spaghetti in the sauce, turn it on to a deep, heated serving dish and sprinkle with the parsley. Cut the partridges in half and arrange them on the spaghetti – there's no need to conceal them, this time!

A crisp and well-chilled salad makes a suitable accompaniment.

---

## POMEGRANATES, RHODES STYLE

### *Rodia se siropi*

If you have ever wondered how to serve pomegranates so that they taste as delicious as they look, read on. I was given this recipe by a lady with a fruit-laden garden, somewhere between Petaloudes, the Valley of the Butterflies, and that marvellous mosaic of social history, the ancient town of Kamiros. Our friend took a stone jar of this sparkling dessert from the refrigerator, where it keeps well for weeks, although it is actually nicer served at room temperature. That way you can pretend the fruit is still warm from the setting sun.

### SERVES 4

*3 pomegranates*
*100g (4oz) sugar*
*a strip of thinly pared orange peel*
*1 tbsp orange juice*
*2 tbsp orange-flower water*

Cut the fruit in half and scoop out the seeds. Separate them from the white fibres that surround them and put them in a bowl.

Put the sugar into a pan with 250ml (8fl oz) water, the orange peel and orange juice. Stir over a low heat to dissolve the sugar, then fast-boil for about 5 minutes until the syrup becomes, well,

syrupy. Remove the pan from the heat, discard the orange peel and stir in the orange-flower water.

Pour the syrup over the pomegranate seeds, mix well, cover and set aside, or chill in the refrigerator, overnight.

Serve in small white china bowls that will show off the glowing ruby-red dessert at its most enticing. Decorate each bowl if you like (although the Greeks don't) with scented herb leaves, such as lemon- or rose-scented geranium.

## Rosemary

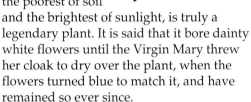

Rosemary, a hardy shrub that thrives in the poorest of soil and the brightest of sunlight, is truly a legendary plant. It is said that it bore dainty white flowers until the Virgin Mary threw her cloak to dry over the plant, when the flowers turned blue to match it, and have remained so ever since.

In Greece, rosemary is familiarly seen as large, dense bushes growing wild by the sea – the Latin name means 'foam of the sea' – and cultivated outside cottage doorways. According to another legend, it will never grow taller than the height of Christ when He was on earth.

The ancient Greeks used the herb in religious ceremonies and in both public and private festivities, burning it like incense. Later, because it was thought to enhance the memory, it became a symbol of fidelity and was used at weddings.

It is one of the most powerful of bee-attracting plants, and rosemary honey is especially good. Greek cooks use the herb sparingly, sometimes adding a sprig or two to casseroles, to fish for baking, and to fruit syrup and preserves. But they are generous in its use in other ways, and you will often see a bunch of the grey-green spiky stems in full flower, hanging in a kitchen or living-room to repel insects and serve as an air freshener.

*Top: Fishing is a family business on all the islands.
Here, children on Astypalea help with the nets.
Above: Ecclesiastical and agricultural architecture in harmony
on Kalymnos. Right: A moment of quiet contemplation in a
medieval setting on Patmos.*

# Yoghurt

I have watched yoghurt being made in Greece at sunrise with milk fresh from a goat and enjoyed it, still warm, sprinkled with olive oil and chopped herbs, at sundown. I have seen yoghurt production in factories where the conditions are scientifically controlled and every batch is identical – and delicious. And I have made it myself, at home and on many a Greek island, in everything from an earthenware flower pot to an electric appliance purpose-made for the job. And still yoghurt is my favourite food on earth!

The story goes that yoghurt was first discovered by nomadic tribesmen who carried fresh milk from one camp to the next in bags made from the lining of sheeps' stomachs, containers that had not been favoured by any process of sterilization. The milk, subjected to both the friendly activities of the inherent bacteria and the warmth of the sun, solidified and, because they were the right bacteria, was preserved, without turning sour.

The principle is simple. Yoghurt is made of two types of bacteria: *Lactobacillus bulgaricus*, which grows most avidly at temperatures between 45 and 47°C (113–117°F), and *Streptococcus thermophilus*, which is most prolific between 37 and 42°C (99–108°F). All you have to do to provide the ideal nursery conditions in which both types of bacteria will readily multiply is to heat the milk, stir in the yoghurt culture and keep it warm.

You can use any type of milk – sheeps', goats', cows', even asses' if you happen to be in the part of the world they inhabit – and you can use pasteurized or unpasteurized milk; homogenized and ultra-heat-treated milk; powdered milk mixed with water according to the instructions on the drum; canned evaporated milk diluted with water; skimmed or semi-skimmed milk (though don't expect to make a rich, creamy yoghurt); and, for special occasions, single or even double cream. The only type of milk that has given me disappointing, not to say disastrous results was frozen goats' milk that I had bought from a local farm.

And as for the culture, you can use a spoonful of any plain, unflavoured, home-made or bought yoghurt, or a sachet of Bulgarian-style yoghurt culture, which is sold in powdered form.

Unless it has already been sterilized, bring the milk to boiling point and leave it to cool to just above blood heat, around 43°C (110°F). At this temperature, if you hold a scrupulously clean finger in the milk while you slowly count to 10, your finger will start to tingle. Allow about 10ml (1 heaped teaspoon) of yoghurt to each 600ml (1 pint) of milk. Mix it thoroughly with a little of the warm milk, then gradually stir in the remaining milk. Use the powdered culture according to the directions on the packet.

Pour the milk into a single sterilized container or several small ones – used yoghurt pots are ideal, of course – cover and set aside at warm room temperature, such as in an airing cupboard or on top of a boiler, for about 8 hours. Another way of ensuring a constant and propitious temperature is to make the yoghurt in a vacuum flask, and another, more accurate still, is to use one of the many types of electric maker now on the market.

Once the yoghurt has set, you can store it in the refrigerator for up to about five days. Leave it any longer and it tends to separate, and should not, then, be used as a starter for the next batch.

# APRICOT PRESERVE

## *Verikoko glyko*

Staying with a village family within energetic walking distance of Rhodes town, we fell into a pleasant domestic routine. My husband spent the mornings up in the mountains with the man of the house, collecting sage leaves to make a dusty tea – they drink it to ward off winter's ills – while I helped to prepare home-grown apricots and stirred cauldrons of jam.

Breakfast every day consisted of home-made bread, this preserve, plain cake and yoghurt accompanied by the song of the birds twittering in the vines. Not a bad life!

## MAKES ABOUT 2kg (4½lb)

*1·5kg (3 ½ lb) apricots*
*75g (3oz) blanched split almonds*
*2 lemons*
*2 tsp allspice berries, crushed*
*1·5kg (3½lb) sugar*
*80ml (3fl oz) brandy*

Halve the apricots and remove the stones. Put them in a pan with the almonds, the juice of the lemons and 450ml (¾ pint) water. Cut up the lemon rind, tie it in a piece of muslin with the allspice berries and add it to the pan.

Bring to the boil and simmer for about 20 minutes until the fruit is tender.

Warm the sugar and add it to the pan. Stir over a low heat to dissolve the sugar, then increase the heat and fast-boil for 10–15 minutes until the preserve will set. Remove and discard the muslin bag and stir in the brandy.

Pour the preserve into clean, warm jars. Cover with waxed paper discs and transparent paper or screw-on covers, label and store them in a cool, dark, dry place.

# QUINCE PASTE

## *Kothonopasto*

Speeding through the Karpathian countryside on bicycles, just outside the fascinating old-style village of Piles, we were hailed by a man who appeared to be winnowing seed. At least, he was shaking a large sieve vigorously from side to side. But no. This was the way, the only efficient way, he told us, of ridding prickly pears of those cruelly spiteful little spikes. His wife turned the now-harmless, sunset-coloured fruits into a thick, chewy paste studded with blanched almonds and enjoyed, always, with ice-cold water. Not having a local prickly pear supplier, I have used quinces, another prolific island crop, instead.

## MAKES ABOUT 1·5kg (3½lb)

*1kg (2¼lb) quinces, peeled, cored and sliced*
*1kg (2¼lb) sugar*
*225g (8oz) blanched split almonds*
*icing sugar to dust (optional)*

Put the quinces in a large saucepan with 1 litre (1¾ pints) water and cook them until they are tender, mashing them frequently to break them up. Liquidize them in a blender or food processor to make a smooth purée.

Return the purée to the cleaned pan and cook over low heat, stirring frequently, for about 30 minutes until it is almost dry.

Warm the sugar and gradually stir it into the purée. Stir over low heat until the sugar has dissolved. Continue cooking and stirring from time to time until the purée is so thick that a wooden spoon drawn through it momentarily parts the preserve into two sections. This stage may take 1–1½ hours.

When the preserve is thick, translucent and a deep coral colour, pour it into a lightly oiled Swiss roll tin, 33 x 22cm (13 x 9in). Stud the top with split almonds and leave to set.

To serve, cut into small diamonds and, if you like, dust the top with icing sugar

# CHAPTER 4

# Crete

Crete, which has been continuously inhabited since Neolithic times, has its own culinary tale to tell – several tales, in fact, since the mountain ranges form sharp cultural as well as geographical divides.

The Lasithi Plain, with its landscape of whirring windmills, is a fertile basket of fruit, nuts and vegetables, with regional dishes, including colour-bright vegetable pizzas, to match. The eastern part is a tropical paradise, where the only natural date grove in Europe exotically fringes the sandy beaches, hands of green-speckled bananas are sold straight from the trees, and glasshouses stretch for miles. Salads, vegetables and a brisk export trade are specialities. The mountainous western region, a maze of rushing streams and shaded valleys, is a hide-and-seek of strung-out villages and isolated farms, the kind where hand-fed pork is the dish of the day. I give one such recipe on page 68.

History is all around you on the island, not only as you explore the awe-inspiring ancient cities and palaces – including Phaistos, Tilissos and Agia Triada – but in the homes, too. Near Heraklion we were overtaken by a rickety truck swaying with huge, decorated, pottery storage jars, urn-shaped *pithari* that were identical to those excavated in the storage chambers in the Palace of Knossos. We saw their like again in a cottage in Aghios Ionnis, in the Amari Valley, where two of our friends – we met them years ago, when we stopped to admire their garden – have a long tunnel of waist-high jars filled with their own wine, oil, olives and wheat and covered, simply, with wooden boards. Rabbits scamper among the jars, chickens scratch for the scattered grain and pigeons and doves come and go

as they please. It's a centuries-old domestic scene that, because of the jars, our friends call 'Knossos'. Hence the name of the recipe on page 72. The hard part, of course (apart from witnessing the demise of our lunch-time rabbit), comes in trying to repay such open-hearted Cretan hospitality without giving offence. It's just about possible to leave

*Opposite: Prawn Pancakes; recipe on page 61.*
*Below: The market at Chania, on Crete, sets out the most tempting of local produce.*

behind a taste of England and a taste of Scotland as if they are parcels you have forgotten in the heat of the moment.

Another visit, another village, a hilltop settlement honeycombed by caves; useful lookouts, we were told, in times of war. It was the last day of our stay, and Maria, her mother and her grandmother had prepared a farewell lunch. As we sat on benches in the one-room cottage, dimmed by the intensity of the sunlight outside, we were offered slices of *mizithra* cheese with sweet, spicy bread, spiky lamb cutlets scented with wild herbs and cooked on an open fire, okra in tomatoes, a mixed country salad covered with feta and glistening with oil, pistachio halva, honey cakes and home-made rosé wine. 'Do you know,' said Maria as we emerged on to the terrace, 'my family has probably been serving that very same kind of meal, made from their own produce, for, oh, hundreds of years?'

---

## PICKLED ARTICHOKE HEARTS

### *Aginares toursi*

Our favourite taverna just outside Fourfouras has a most unusual star attraction on the counter – a huge jar of pickled artichoke hearts.

These tender and tangy, not quite yellow, not quite green, vegetables are served by the appetizing plateful, while customers sit under the vines and wait as thyme-scattered joints of baby goat sizzle on the barbecue. They feature prominently in a salad with Cos lettuce, black olives and spring onions, and in another with hot-as-mustard grilled red peppers drizzled with oil and local red wine. They are served as a piquant garnish to grilled fish and, if you sit there long enough, they will be offered again, as a digestive after the meal, with *raki* or brandy.

*12 very young artichokes*
*6 tbsp lemon juice*
*salt*
*1 tsp dried oregano*
*about 150ml (¹/₄ pint) red wine*
*about 150ml (¹/₄ pint) olive oil*

Have ready a large bowl of water, acidulated with 2 tbsp of the lemon juice, to prevent the artichokes from discolouring.

Pull off the tough outer leaves of the artichokes. Open out the vegetables and scrape away the fluffy choke in the centre – a teaspoon is useful for this. Trim the remaining leaves close to the heart and cut off the stalk. Work as quickly as you can and immediately drop each prepared vegetable into the bowl of water and lemon juice.

When all the artichokes have been prepared, bring a large pan of salted water to the boil and add 2 tbsp of the remaining lemon juice. Partly cook the artichokes at a fast, rolling boil for 3 minutes. It may be most convenient to do this in two batches. Transfer them to a bowl of fresh, cold water and leave them to cool.

Drain and dry the artichokes and slice them thinly, through the leaves and the heart or base. Pack them in a sterilized jar, sprinkling each layer with the remaining lemon juice and the oregano. Pour on the red wine and olive oil to cover the artichokes – the exact amount you need will depend on the relative volumes of the vegetables and the container.

Close the jar tightly – a screw-on lid is ideal – and shake it over and over to blend the wine and oil. Set aside for at least 4 weeks before using.

## PRAWN PANCAKES

*Crockettes me garithes*

The bad news was that our hired car had broken down in Ierapetra, the coastal town that services Crete's most prolific horticultural region, towards the southeast of the island.

The good news came when the garage mechanic recommended us to his own favourite fish restaurant, Napoleon the Great, almost at the end of a long, long ribbon of tavernas, restaurants and bars that forms a gastronomic *tour de force* between the beach and the high road.

The proprietor brought us this speciality of the house, known as *crockettes*, before the main course.

### SERVES 4

*125g (5oz) plain flour*
*salt*
*2 large eggs, beaten*
*350ml (12fl oz) lukewarm milk*
*1 tbsp olive oil*
*2 tbsp chopped parsley*
*75g (3oz) butter*
*1 medium onion, finely chopped*
*4 cloves garlic, finely chopped*
*½ green pepper, cored, seeded and chopped*
*½ red pepper, cored, seeded and chopped*
*225g (8oz) shelled prawns, roughly chopped*
*black pepper*

To make the pancake batter, sift the flour and salt into a bowl, make a well in the centre and pour in the eggs. Stir the eggs into the flour, then gradually pour on the milk, beating constantly to make a smooth batter. Stir in the oil and chopped parsley. Or put everything, except the parsley, into a blender or food processor and whizz it into submission. Stir in the chopped parsley.

Melt 50g (2oz) of the butter in an omelette pan and fry the onion over medium heat until it is transparent. Add the garlic and chopped peppers and fry for about 3 minutes more until the peppers begin to soften. Turn the mixture into a bowl, stir in the prawns and season with pepper.

Melt one quarter of the remaining butter in the pan. When it is hot, swirl it around and add one quarter of the prawn mixture. Pour over one quarter of the batter, tip the pan to spread it evenly and cook for 2–3 minutes, until the mixture is set. Toss the pancake and cook it on the other side for 2–3 minutes until it is light brown. Slide the pancake on to a heated plate and keep it warm while you cook the remainder in the same way. Serve hot.

These pancakes are specially tasty served with *skorthalia* (garlic sauce, see page 45) .

## Raki

Almost every country has its national distillation, the local 'fire water', which visitors imbibe freely at their peril. It may be distilled from any one of a variety of ingredients – rice, grapes, milk, sugar-cane, dates and palm sap to name but a few – and it is known by a variety of names, *marc* and *arrack* among them.

In Greece such a spirit is known as *raki* – *tsipouro* on Crete – and it is distilled from the wine-making left-overs, the pulpy residue of skins, stalks and pips left in the press after the juice has been taken off. It may, for all I know, vary from place to place in intensity and degrees proof, but since it is often served from unlabelled bottles, it is hard to tell.

A small glass of *raki* may well be offered with coffee and a spoon sweet as part of the traditional welcome when you are invited into a Greek home. The custom is to drink it in one gulp, but I don't think one would give offence by taking a few discreet sips, as long as they were compensated for by a suitably appreciative smile.

Making *raki* is a thriving cottage industry throughout the islands, and you may well hear the tell-tale clank of bottles or observe the smoke from the boiler as you pass a farm outhouse after the grape harvest. Then the family's gesture of hospitality may be a good deal less formal. I don't pretend to have a discerning palate when it comes to different *raki* vintages, but a sip from a tin can dipped in a vat and passed around the group – it was in a courtyard on Karpathos, actually – tasted pretty good to me.

# The Taverna

In popular holiday areas you will be able to take your pick from tavernas where the canned or live music is at least as important as the food; from ones where the 'action' starts when the waiters take time off from serving to instruct the customers in the intricate art of *sirtaki* dancing; and – if you are lucky – from one or two small, family-run establishments in the less fashionable parts of town, where the only music is provided by a radio or cassette player.

Such tavernas, where a limited range of food is served simply, as it might be in a Greek home, require persistence and a few discreet enquiries to track down. When you do find one, don't be put off by the odd chip of peeling paint. As like as not, the kitchen will be spotless.

Anyway, you will see this for yourself. It is usual for customers to inspect the food in the kitchen, nodding approvingly as the proprietor lifts the lid of an aluminium pan of lamb casserole or macaroni in tomato sauce, or indicates a row of meat-filled vegetables on a hotplate.

Meat and fish for grilling and pan-frying will usually be kept in a cold cabinet in full view of the diners and – depending on the size of the taverna and its day-to-day selection – you will be invited to make your choice from pork chops, steak and veal cutlets; from red mullet, smelts (*marithes*), swordfish steaks and so on. Don't be surprised if you are asked how much fish you want – in tavernas it is often sold by weight, rather than by any predetermined portion size.

'Popular' tavernas usually offer a range of openers (*mezethes*) such as the ever-favourite cods' roe pâté (*taramosalata*), but the smaller 'local' ones usually do not. As soon as you sit down, the proprietor or a waiter will bring a plastic cloth to cover the table, a basket of chunky bread and your choice of wine. Those in the know will ask for retsina from a barrel in the shop. If there is a menu, it will have two price columns. You will be charged the higher one, which includes the tourist tax.

Desserts don't always figure on the menus of small tavernas, and some don't even serve coffee. So after your meal it may be a case of adjourning to a *kafenion* for a coffee and a brandy, or a pastry shop (*zacharoplasteion*) to add a cream cake or pastry to your enjoyment.

*Left: The party gets into full swing – impromptu dancing in a beachside taverna on Kalymnos. Above: Bright lights and tables ringing the harbour are a magnetic attraction at Rethymnon, Crete.*

## VINEYARD FISH

### Psari me stafilia

It was one of those walk-back-in-time days when we had been entranced all over again by the regal ruins of ancient Phaistos and nearby Agia Triada where, incidentally, I always buy my dried oregano. (Well, the twinkling old stallholder has such a good line in culinary patter.) The excursion finished on a high note, with this dish bringing together two significant local harvests.

### SERVES 4–6

50g (2oz) butter
2 medium onions, finely chopped
2 cloves garlic, finely chopped
1kg (2¼lb) sea bream, cleaned, scaled, washed and dried
2 bay leaves
300ml (½ pint) white wine, or 150ml (¼ pint) dry vermouth and 150ml (¼ pint) water
salt and black pepper
2 egg yolks
juice of 2 lemons
2 tsp cornflour
225g (8oz) seedless white grapes
2 tbsp double cream
1 tbsp chopped parsley
lemon wedges, to serve

Melt the butter in a large flameproof dish and fry the onion over medium heat until it is transparent. Add the garlic and fry for 1–2 minutes more. (If you do not have a suitable flameproof dish, soften the onion and garlic in a small pan and transfer it to an ovenproof dish.)

Place the fish on the onion mixture, add the bay leaves and pour on the wine. Season with salt and pepper, cover the dish and bake in the oven at 190°C (375°F/Gas 5) for 35–40 minutes, until the fish is just firm.

Transfer the fish to a heated serving dish, cover it with foil and keep it warm.

Discard the bay leaves and pour the fish liquid into a small pan. Beat together the egg yolks and lemon juice. Mix the cornflour to a smooth paste with 2 tbsp water and stir in a little of the hot fish stock. Pour the cornflour and the egg mixture into the pan, add the grapes and stir over low heat until the sauce begins to thicken. Do not allow it to boil. Stir in the cream, taste and adjust the seasoning if necessary.

Pour the sauce over the fish, sprinkle on the parsley and serve with lemon wedges.

Plain boiled potatoes go well with this dish – cut them into quarters lengthways for Greek authenticity. Alternatively, you could serve rice tossed with a handful of slivered almonds and a little chopped parsley.

---

## FRUIT PLATE

### Frouta tis Kritis

I love harvest-time in Crete, not so much the golden wheat harvest, evocative though that is, but the sunshine-gold and mellow fruit crop of, well, take your pick, apricots, peaches, oranges, cherries. In some island homes a plate of mixed fruits, tinglingly, icily cold and sparkling with drops of water is served as a first course, before the vegetables, the meat or fish and, if you're lucky, the halva. Oh, I nearly forgot to mention – the secret lies in the *raki*.

### SERVES 4

450g (1lb) ripe apricots, halved and stoned
4 or 8 peaches, depending on size, stoned and quartered
4 small, thin-skinned oranges, peeled and segmented
225g (8oz) seedless white grapes
4 or 8 tbsp raki, chilled, or use white rum
4 sprigs of herb, to decorate

Chill all the fruit and the plates well in advance of serving. This really does make all the difference.

Divide the fruits among four individual serving plates, arranging them in a symmetrical pattern. To do this well, as so many island cooks do, is an art form in itself. Sprinkle the fruit on each plate with 1 or 2 tbsp of the spirit and decorate it with a sprig of herb. I like to use purple basil for the unlikely but effective colour combination.

# SQUID, RETHYMNON STYLE

*Kalamarakia Rethymnou*

Dining out in the harbour at Rethymnon is a leisurely, watching-the-world-go-by experience – once you have perused all the menus, exchanged pavement pleasantries with the hard-selling waiters and, finally, made your choice from the clatter of competing tavernas, that is.

We were on our way to spend Easter with friends in the south and stopped off to enjoy this traditional Lenten dish. By coincidence, it cropped up again in the first meal we were offered, in a private house, at our next port of call.

### SERVES 4

*1kg (2¼lb) squid (kalamares)*
*8 tbsp olive oil*
*3 medium onions, sliced*
*2 cloves garlic, finely chopped*
*2 large 'beef' tomatoes, peeled and chopped,*
*or 225g (8oz) canned tomatoes, chopped*
*150ml (¼ pint) white wine*
*2 tbsp chopped parsley*
*salt and black pepper*
*175g (6oz) long-grain rice, washed and drained*
*lemon wedges, to serve*

Prepare the squid by washing thoroughly. Remove the ink bag, head, entrails and tentacles, and pull out the transparent backbone. Cut into 5cm (2in) pieces and wash again.

Heat the oil in a large pan and fry the onions over medium heat until they are transparent. Add the garlic and fry for 1–2 minutes more.

Add the squid to the pan, stir well and cook for 4–5 minutes, stirring once or twice. Stir in the tomatoes, pour on the wine, add the parsley and season with salt and pepper. Bring to the boil, cover the pan and simmer for 20 minutes.

Pour on 100ml (4fl oz) water, stir in the rice, cover the pan again and simmer slowly for about 15 minutes until the rice is tender. Stir from time to time to prevent it from sticking. If the liquid dries out during this time, add another 1–2 tbsp water. Taste the rice and add more seasoning if necessary.

Set the covered pan aside in a warm place for 5 minutes before serving. Serve with lemon wedges.

## Lent

In the Greek Orthodox calendar Lent begins on 'Clean Monday', *Kathari Deftera* (see page 29), and continues for the 40 days before Easter Sunday. The interval is not only a time for fasting, when (except for young children and the elderly) the consumption of meat, eggs, butter, cheese and milk is prohibited. It is also a time for religious reflection. As the pressures of spring-cleaning, shopping and food preparation build up, so does the awareness of the solemnity of the occasion. It comes as something of a shock to a visitor in a market to be haggling over the price of a tray of peaches against the background of the deeply liturgical music relayed from every street vendor's stall.

Good Friday, the most solemn day of all, is marked by a four-hour church service during which comings and goings are permitted, and wise grandmothers take a bag of biscuits and cakes for the children. The bell tolls mournfully, and a flower-strewn bier, signifying Christ's journey from the cross, is carried in procession three times around the church.

The congregation goes quietly home to the most frugal meal of the year, for which many families add fish and seafood to the list of prohibited foods, and, the ultimate culinary sacrifice, abstain even from olive oil as well.

We joined one hospitable family for their Good Friday supper in a cottage in Lahanes on Corfu. The meal, set out in advance on a gingham cloth, consisted of cold wild greens lightly simmered in lemon juice, vine leaf parcels filled with rice and currants, butter bean, tomato and onion salad, cold boiled potatoes, a mixed green salad dressed with wine and chopped herbs, olives and, the highlight of the occasion, halva made with sesame seed paste (*tahini*) and semolina.

Wine is permitted and, in common with many village families, our host served a bottle of his most prized home-made vintage, a 21-year-old dry red wine, in honour of the occasion.

## LAMB CUTLETS IN PAPER

*Arnisia paithakia sto harti*

There always seems to be an air of excitement buzzing around Lakki, the little town at the head of what we christened Cherry Valley. Most visitors will be on their way to the legendary Samaria Gorge and, especially for those who are cycling, it promises to be a long haul.

We enjoyed a meal of lamb chops 'bandit style' at one of the tavernas under the ring of fairy lights in the square. It's a culinary reminder that this is, truly, lonely shepherd country.

### SERVES 4–6

*4 tbsp olive oil*
*8–12 lamb cutlets, trimmed of excess fat*
*2 medium onions, chopped*
*2 tbsp tomato purée*
*2 large tomatoes, skinned and chopped*
*3 tbsp chopped coriander or parsley*
*250ml (8fl oz) white wine*
*1 tsp sugar*
*salt and black pepper*
*2 tbsp lemon juice*

Heat the oil in a frying-pan, and fry the cutlets over medium heat to brown them on both sides. Remove the cutlets from the pan.

Fry the onion in the pan until it is transparent, stir in the tomato purée, the tomatoes and the chopped herb and pour on the wine. Mix to a smooth sauce, stir in the sugar and season with salt and pepper. Bring to the boil and simmer until the sauce thickens slightly. Taste and adjust the seasoning if necessary.

Sprinkle the cutlets on both sides with the lemon juice and season them with salt and pepper. Place each cutlet on a square of greaseproof paper and spoon the sauce on top, dividing it evenly among them. Fold over the paper to enclose the cutlets and place the parcels in a single layer in a roasting tin.

Cook the cutlets in the oven at 180°C (350°F/Gas 4) for about 40 minutes until they are tender.

Serve the cutlets in the paper. Part of the fun – and the tradition – of this dish is in unwrapping the

*Pages 66–7: Lamb Cutlets in Paper.*

parcels at the table. The initial waft of herbs and wine promises well for the impregnated flavour of the lamb. Serve with small potatoes in their jackets, baked in the oven at the same time, and with a green vegetable or salad.

---

## PORK WITH CELERIAC

*Hirino me selinorizes avgolemono*

Western Crete is a roller-coaster of deep, deep gorges, blissfully cool even in summer and spectacular in the autumn, when they are set alight by the fiery gold of the plane and chestnut trees. The steep hillsides are meticulously cultivated with patchwork strips of wheat, and, in parts of the region, the production of olive oil is a prime and air-pervading industry.

Somewhere, exploring our way west to east on an uncharted route, we found accommodation and gratefully sat down to a hearty farmhouse stew of home-raised pork and garden vegetables.

### SERVES 4

*4 tbsp olive oil*
*1kg (2¼lb) lean pork, cubed and patted dry*
*2 medium onions, sliced*
*2 cloves garlic, finely chopped*
*600ml (1 pint) chicken stock*
*salt and black pepper*
*450g (1lb) young celeriac, trimmed and scraped*
*2 tbsp vinegar*
*2 eggs*
*juice of 2 lemons*
*2 tsp cornflour*
*2 tbsp chopped parsley*
*lemon wedges, to serve (optional)*

Heat the oil in a large pan and fry the pork cubes over medium heat until they are lightly and evenly brown on all sides. It may be necessary to do this in two batches as it is important not to crowd the meat. Lift out the meat with a draining spoon and set it aside.

Fry the onion in the pan until it is transparent. Add the garlic and fry for 1–2 minutes more. Return the meat to the pan, pour on the stock, season with salt and pepper, stir well and bring slowly to the boil. Cover the pan and simmer for 1 hour.

Meanwhile, cook the celeriac in a large pan of boiling water with the vinegar and some salt for about 15 minutes or until it is just beginning to soften. Drain the vegetable, leave it to cool for a while, then slice it or cut it into cubes.

Add the celeriac to the pan, stir well, cover the pan and simmer for about 20 minutes, until both the meat and the celeriac are tender.

Beat together the eggs and lemon juice. Mix the cornflour to a smooth paste with 2 tbsp water and stir it into the egg mixture. Add a little of the meat sauce, stir it well and pour the mixture into the pan. Stir it over low heat until it just begins to thicken, but do not allow the sauce to boil – which would have a disastrous effect on the texture. Taste the sauce and adjust the seasoning if necessary.

Sprinkle with the parsley and serve with lemon wedges if you like.

You can't beat plain boiled potatoes with an unpretentious dish like this.

*   *   *

If you can't buy celeriac, try using thickly sliced fennel instead. Blanch it for only 4–5 minutes before adding it to the meat and use the chopped leaves for garnish.

# CHICKEN BREASTS WITH FETA CHEESE

*Kotopoulo me feta*

Agia Galini is a cosmopolitan little fishing village south of the Amari Valley. It's a happy hunting ground for anyone who, like me, collects those state-of-the-photographic-art scenic postcards and who loves to sit under an umbrella demolishing snowy mountains of exotic ice-creams.

The menus in the tavernas and restaurants owe little to local tradition, more to their international clientele, but this recipe from one of them is worth noting.

### SERVES 4

*a handful of spinach leaves*
*salt*
*4 chicken breasts (about 200g (7oz) each)*
*100g (4oz) feta cheese*
*black pepper*
*75g (3oz) butter*
*2 tbsp flour*
*150ml (¼ pint) white wine*
*150ml (¼ pint) chicken stock*
*2 tbsp chopped coriander or parsley*
*4 tbsp double cream*

Remove any thick stalks from the spinach and blanch the leaves in boiling, salted water for 2 minutes. Drain in a colander and pat the leaves dry with kitchen paper.

Cut a deep slit horizontally in each chicken breast, but do not cut it right through. Pack the openings with the spinach leaves and crumbled or sliced feta cheese and season with pepper. Press the chicken together again to make a tight sandwich.

Melt the butter in a frying-pan and fry the chicken over medium heat for 4–5 minutes on each side, until it is golden brown. Remove the chicken, and keep it warm.

Stir the flour into the butter and, when it has formed a roux, gradually pour on the wine and stock, stirring all the time. Bring the sauce to the boil, stir in the coriander or parsley and return the chicken to the pan. Spoon the sauce over the meat, cover the pan and simmer for 30 minutes, turning the chicken once.

Stir in the cream, taste the sauce and adjust the seasoning if necessary.

Serve with rice or noodles and a crisp, well-chilled salad.

*Overleaf: The harbour at Plakias, southern Crete.*

## The First of May

May takes its name from Maia, the mother of the god Hermes. It is considered the most beautiful month of the year in Greece, a view to which anyone who has wandered through fields dappled with the dazzling pink and white, yellow and mauve flowers of spring will happily testify.

*Protomayia*, the first day of May, ushering in this hallowed month, has, therefore, a special significance and is celebrated as a festival of spring and youth and, at a practical level, as a festival of flowers.

As on so many high days and holidays in Greece, people arm themselves with a generous picnic and take to the countryside for a day of family celebration. Tradition has it that they gather handfuls of wild flowers, which they bind into a wreath, known as a *stefani*, to hang on the door when they get home. Nowadays, however, many people make their garlands from wild or garden flowers on the eve of the festival and hang them up in readiness for the forthcoming day.

It may be an all-white and restrained hoop of daisy-like marguerites, a multi-coloured ring fashioned from mixed bunches, like a random floral patchwork, or an artistic design in carefully selected shades. But whatever the floral composition of the wreath, the superstitious will add a head of garlic to ward off the evil eye.

Don't be surprised if, travelling around the islands some weeks after the festival, you see these door wreaths looking somewhat the sadder for the passage of time. In some regions, the wreaths will be left to hang on the doors for several weeks and then ritually burned in the garden or on the street. Members of the family – principally the children, now – are invited to jump three times over the ashes, wishing for good luck as they do so.

## RABBIT, KNOSSOS STYLE

*Kouneli Knossou*

Maria and Alexandros, whose tiny cottage is set in the heart of their olive grove, cook this dish over a roaring wood fire in the corner of their living room. The oil spits, the wine hisses and the heat becomes unbearable, but it's all in a good cause – the rabbit is deliciously tender. The heart and liver are cooked on a skewer over the flame and offered to guests separately, as a signal of welcome.

As the rabbit joints are customarily eaten in the fingers – and the bones gnawed until they are white – elegance and pretty table manners give way to conviviality and shared relish.

### SERVES 4

*1 young rabbit, jointed, offal reserved*
*salt and black pepper*
*1–2 tbsp dried oregano*
*8 tbsp olive oil*
*150ml (¼ pint) full-bodied red wine*

Wash and dry the rabbit joints, the heart and the liver and sprinkle them liberally with salt, pepper and oregano.

Heat the oil in a large, heavy-based pan – a cast-iron one is ideal – until it is very hot. Add the rabbit joints and sear them on all sides – long-handled tongs are useful for turning them over and over – until they are lightly coloured. This takes about 15–20 minutes in all. Add the heart and liver and cook them, turning them once or twice, for the last 4–5 minutes.

Remove the pan from the heat and slowly pour on the wine, taking care that it does not splash you. Continue cooking over high heat, turning the meat frequently, until most of the wine has evaporated. Its purpose is to flavour the meat not to provide a sauce.

Cut up the heart and liver into small pieces and serve them on cocktail sticks as an appetizer, one for each person.

The traditional way to eat the rabbit is in the fingers. Finger bowls are unheard of in country villages – the kitchen sink is never very far away – but if you plan to adopt the local custom, they would certainly be welcome.

# MIXED VEGETABLES IN EGG AND LEMON SAUCE

*Lahanika anamikta avgolemono*

Maria, our hostess in Thronos, that heavenly hilltop village at the head of the Amari valley, described herself as 'almost a vegetarian'. And so day after day we grew to appreciate the mix and match of flavours, textures and colours that could be achieved in a dish of mixed vegetables gathered, she insisted, from her garden only moments before cooking. In country homes such a dish would be served with chunks of coarse brown bread soaked in water until it is crumbly and then dipped in oil.

### SERVES 4

*4 young globe artichokes*
*4 tbsp lemon juice*
*salt*
*450g (1lb) potatoes, peeled*
*350g (12oz) carrots, trimmed and scraped*
*450g (1lb) broad beans, shelled, or use 225g (8oz)*
*frozen beans, thawed*
*2 small heads fennel, trimmed*
*3 tbsp finely chopped fennel leaves*
*lemon wedges, to serve (optional)*

### SAUCE
*juice of 3 lemons*
*4 egg yolks*
*black pepper*

Prepare the globe artichokes as described on page 60 and drop them at once into water acidulated with 2 tbsp of the lemon juice. Drain the artichokes and cook them in a pan of boiling, salted water with the remaining 2 tbsp lemon juice for about 35 minutes or until the hearts, or bases, are tender. Drain them thoroughly on kitchen paper, then set them aside, keeping them warm.

Meanwhile, cook the potatoes, carrots, broad beans and fennel in separate pans of boiling, salted water until they are just tender. If the dish is to be as delicious as Maria's, all the vegetables should have a distinct 'bite' to them. Drain the vegetables and reserve the liquid, measuring 350ml (12fl oz) into a small pan.

Slice the artichokes thinly through the leaves and hearts. Cut the potatoes in quarters lengthways and the carrots into finger strips – halve them if they are unmanageably long. Slice the fennel lengthways. Combine all the vegetables and keep them warm in a heated serving dish while you make the sauce.

Whisk the lemon juice and egg yolks and beat in about 4 tbsp of the reserved vegetable stock. Pour this into the hot stock in the pan, season with pepper and heat the sauce gently, without boiling. As soon as it starts to thicken, taste it and adjust the seasoning if necessary. Pour the sauce over the vegetables, toss them carefully and sprinkle with the chopped fennel leaves. Serve, if you wish, with lemon wedges.

## Oregano

It might be tactful to allow Theophrastus, the ancient Greek herbalist, to introduce the plant, which is popularly known as Cretan dittany. 'This plant,' he wrote, 'is marvellous in virtue and is useful for many purposes, but especially for women in childbirth.... If goats eat it when they have been shot, it rids them of the arrow.' He went on to explain that bunches of dittany inserted into the hollow stems of giant fennel will ensure that it 'may not exhale its virtue'.

One comes across the plant growing wild in mountainous regions all over Greece, but especially in Crete, its highly pungent leaves and clusters of pink flowers contrasting prettily with the rocky terrain. And one comes across the dried leaves, in bulging packets labelled *rigani*, on many of the islands, too. Buy plenty. I wouldn't be without my stocks of dried oregano, which, as you can see from many of the recipes, I have learned to use almost as frequently as salt and pepper.

When I was travelling in the islands researching for an earlier book, I became somewhat engrossed in the subject of herbs and talked to a wide cross-section of regional cooks on the subject. The received wisdom was that dried oregano retains its flavour more satisfactorily than any other herb, even thyme, with which it is usually interchangeable.

*Left: Gathering wild greens,* horta, *in the lush and fertile plains near Phaistos. The leaves are cooked like spinach. Top: A discussion of current affairs punctuates a Cretan journey. Above: Richly decorated wedding breads with traditional floral motifs await the celebrations.*

## OKRA IN TOMATO SAUCE

*Bamies me saltsa domatas*

Okra is a popular vegetable in Cretan homes, but it is not instantly acclaimed by visitors. Perhaps this is because everyone seems to have at least one uncomplimentary okra experience to relate – you know, the 'school dinners' kind of experience, which is guaranteed to put you off some kinds of food for life.

My reservations about okra were finally overcome in an island home where the fresh, young vegetables were simply cooked in a sharp tomato sauce and served with pan-fried lamb chops and the inevitable plate of chips.

### SERVES 4–6

*750g (1½ lb) young okra, washed and trimmed*
*100ml (4fl oz) vinegar*
*salt*
*150ml (¼ pint) olive oil*
*1 medium onion, chopped*
*5 cloves garlic, finely chopped*
*2 tbsp tomato purée*
*450g (1lb) canned tomatoes, chopped*
*2 tbsp lemon juice*
*black pepper*
*6 tbsp chopped coriander or parsley*
*lemon wedges, to serve*

Arrange the okra in a single layer in a shallow dish. Pour over the vinegar and sprinkle with salt. Set aside for about 2 hours. Drain the okra, discarding the vinegar, and wash it well.

Heat a little of the oil in a large pan and fry the onion over medium heat until it is transparent. Add the garlic and fry for 1 minute more. Stir in the tomato purée, add the tomatoes, the lemon juice and the remaining oil, and season with salt and pepper.

Bring the sauce to the boil, stir well and simmer, uncovered, for 15 minutes.

Stir in 5 tbsp of the chopped herb. Add the okra to the pan, spoon the sauce over the vegetable and simmer, uncovered, for about 20 minutes, until the okra is tender and there is no excess moisture in the sauce. By now it should be like a thick paste.

Sprinkle the dish with the remaining herb and serve warm or cold, with lemon wedges.

---

## MIXED WILD GREENS

*Horta anamikta*

All over Greece villagers take to the hills with great enthusiasm to pick a selection of leafy greens to serve as a separate course or, less often, as an accompaniment to the main dish. The success – to state the obvious – lies in the cooking. The leaves must be only lightly and partially cooked, so that each type retains its individual flavour.

With no Cretan mountainside on your doorstep, you can make more than a passable attempt at the dish with spinach, sorrel, chard and young dandelion leaves.

### SERVES 4

*about 750g (1½ lb) mixed green leaves, washed and drained*
*salt*
*4 tbsp lemon juice*
*about 8 tbsp olive oil*
*black pepper*
*lemon wedges, to serve*

Remove any tough ribs or stalks. Cook the leaves in one or two large pans of boiling, salted water for 3 minutes, until they are just tender. Turn the leaves into a colander, shake them up and down to remove excess moisture and pat them dry with kitchen paper. Pools of cooking water are not what this dish is all about.

Transfer the leaves to a heated serving dish, sprinkle them with the lemon juice and oil and be generous with the black pepper. Toss the leaves as you would for a salad. Serve warm with lemon wedges.

# POACHED APPLES

## *Mila krasata*

There's more than a hint of the tropics about Vai, on the east wing of the island, a region blissfully fanned by the warm African wind and luxuriant with date palm groves and banana plantations.

Over supper one night a hospitable and venerable priest treated us to a vivid word picture of his wife treading grapes in their bed frame – just the right size, he explained, for their annual harvest. His good lady produced many a glass of the product of her labours – a thick, sweet wine rather like Madeira – and used it to good effect in this simple dessert.

## SERVES 4

*4 large cooking apples, peeled and cored*
*16 cloves*
*2 small bananas, chopped*
*75g (3oz) sugar*
*250ml (8fl oz) red wine*
*Greek yoghurt, chilled, to serve*

Push four cloves around the top of each apple. Fill the centres with the chopped banana – it may be necessary to scoop out a little more of the apple flesh to make room.

Place the sugar and wine in a pan and bring slowly to the boil, stirring until the sugar has dissolved.

Add the apples to the pan, baste with the wine syrup, cover and simmer for 15–20 minutes until the apples are tender. Baste them with the syrup occasionally. Leave the apples to cool in the syrup.

Serve them in individual bowls, drizzled with the syrup and topped with yoghurt.

---

# KATERINA'S CHOCOLATE CAKE

## *Keik sokolatas tis Katerinas*

We dined one evening with a delightfully ebullient artist at her home in Rethymnon, a single room crammed with family treasures and centuries-old examples of island crafts.

As the wine and *raki* bottles circulated freely, Katerina served large, sticky slices of a rich, moist chocolate cake, the perfect ending to the meal. She was rather shy of parting with the recipe – a closely guarded family secret, no doubt – so this is my version, the closest I can get to a memorably delicious flavour and texture.

## SERVES 8–10

*175g (6oz) plain or bitter chocolate*
*2 tsp instant coffee granules*
*2 tbsp boiling water*
*5 eggs, separated*
*175g (6oz) caster sugar*
*225g (8oz) black cherry jam, plus extra for serving (optional)*
*300ml (½ pint) Greek yoghurt, to serve*
*icing sugar, to dust*

Line the bases of two 20cm (8in) sandwich tins with silicone paper.

Break the chocolate into pieces and melt it in a bowl over a pan of simmering water. Dissolve the coffee in the boiling water and stir it into the chocolate. Leave to cool. Beat the egg yolks and sugar until the mixture becomes pale and syrupy. Pour into the chocolate mixture and beat until it is evenly distributed.

Whisk the egg whites until they are stiff but not dry. Fold them into the chocolate mixture until they, too, have been evenly mixed. Pour the mixture into the prepared sandwich tins and bake in the centre of a pre-heated oven at 180°C (350°F/Gas 4) for 20–25 minutes. Test the cake for 'doneness' by inserting a skewer in the centre. It should come out clean.

Allow the layers to cool in the tins for a few minutes, then turn them out to finish cooling on a wire rack. Spread one layer with the jam and assemble the cake. Sprinkle the top with icing sugar, which Katerina calls 'the snow on the Idi mountains'.

Serve the cake with heaped spoonfuls of yoghurt and, if you like to be indulgent, more cherry jam.

# CHAPTER 5

# The Northeast Aegean

Ikaria, which has the appearance of a near-tropical garden, abounding in apricots, pears, almonds and grapes, and with a strong and distinctive line in *raki*, made from the arbutus berry; equally green Samos, with its cascading streams, cool, clear springs, olive groves and ancient vineyards; Chios, or Hios, with the heady aroma of orange and tangerine blossom and its sweet-scented honey; Lesbos, with its inland cattle farms (and remarkably good steaks), its scrub-covered fields rustling with wild fowl and, at Plomari, a sizeable ouzo factory; Lemnos or, again, Limnos, with its honey-flavoured Muscat wine, crystallized fruits and (a puff-ball sight in summer) its cotton fields; Samothrace, rising to impressive peaks, with its abundant wheat harvest and all the traditional celebrations that go with it; and Thassos, an outsider in this group (it is actually an offshore island of Thessalonika), with its lines of pale blue beehives brightening the olive groves and producing honey that is the pride of the island (figs and walnuts preserved in it are a delectable speciality) – the islands in the north of the Aegean offer, in food terms, a happy prospect.

My most outstanding meal-oriented memories are of Lesbos, where we stayed close to the southern shore and walked, cycled and chugged our way on motor bikes to the ancient city sites, the petrified forest, the potteries – where you can buy the lovely water jars known as *koumaria* – the never-ending string of fishing villages and the remotest of inland hamlets. And where we strayed off-course several times in the process.

It was the closest we ever came, for one thing, to spending an unscheduled night on a cold, bare mountain. We were foot-sore, hopelessly lost in spite of carrying a compass and clearly miles from home; it was approaching midnight and we had run out of what Pooh Bear calls 'provisions'. It seemed like a miracle when, on the point of giving up, we saw a single light in a forest hut. We were welcomed with open arms, given cold sea bream and chips, wine and blankets, and then breakfast of

*Opposite: Fish Mayonnaise; recipe on page 84.*
*Below: Face to face with mellow stone in a street in Metsa, on Chios.*

bread and honey. And all with not a word of rebuke!

Ikaria comes vividly to mind for quite different reasons. The whole island, carpeted with wild thyme, seems to be a goat farm. Put the two together, as the animals do quite naturally when they graze, and you have the tastiest barbecued meat – and milk – ever.

I turned 'our' kitchen into a working farmhouse in no time at all, with covered earthenware pots of yoghurt on every surface, scalded cloths of yoghurt hanging over bowls to drain off the whey, and blocks of soft, crumbly cheese to enjoy, every now and then, with coarse bread and a glass of wine, *raki* or, another island speciality, apricot brandy. It's called the simple life.

## ROLLED COURGETTE FLOWERS

*Yemista anthi kolokithias*

Impertinent curiosity gets the better of me whenever I see a village housewife taking a tray of food to be cooked in the baker's oven. I just have to know what it is!

Sometimes the cloth will be lifted to reveal the lady's own light-as-a-feather dough. Once it turned out to be figs simmered in honey and wine, and once, on Thassos, it was golden courgette flowers with the irresistible aroma of lemon and herbs. It's a simple recipe, and one that makes a delicious summer appetizer.

### SERVES 4–6

*24 courgette flowers*
*150ml (¼ pint) olive oil*
*2 medium onions, finely chopped*
*100g (4oz) long-grain rice, washed and drained*
*2 tbsp pine nuts*
*75g (3oz) feta cheese, grated or finely chopped*
*2 tbsp chopped parsley*
*salt and black pepper*
*grated nutmeg*
*juice of 2 lemons*
*lemon wedges, to serve*

Open out the courgette flowers (see page 32). Cut off the stamens and any stalk and wash them. Dry them on kitchen paper.

To make the filling, heat about 5 tbsp olive oil in a pan and fry the onion over medium heat until it is transparent. Stir in the rice and cook for 1–2 minutes, until it is well coated with oil. Pour on 300ml (½ pint) water, bring to the boil and cover the pan. Lower the heat and simmer for 15 minutes or until the rice is tender and has absorbed all the water.

Draw the pan away from the heat, stir in the pine nuts, cheese and parsley and season with salt and pepper and a few gratings of nutmeg. Leave the mixture to cool.

Pack the filling into the courgette flowers and roll up each one tightly, starting at the stalk end. Place the rolls in a single layer in a large pan. Pour on the remaining oil, the lemon juice and 150ml (¼ pint) water and shake the pan gently to mix the liquids. Place a large plate over the rolled flowers to keep them immersed in the liquid and cover the pan. Bring the liquid to the boil and simmer very slowly, over low heat, for 1 hour. Remove the pan from the heat and leave it to cool completely, when all the liquid should have been absorbed.

Serve the courgette flower rolls, with lemon wedges, as an appetizer. Chilled ouzo goes rather well with this traditional country dish.

## FRIED CHEESE

*Saganaki*

I remember a late mist-over-the-water evening meal in Kokari, on the northern coast of Samos, not so much for the fried cheese, which was creamily, meltingly delicious, nor even for the smooth, sweet red Samian wine, which has been justly famous since ancient times.

No. This was the occasion when my mathematical conversions deserted me, and I ordered kilos of sizzling, thyme-sprinkled spit-roast goat when I meant to ask, less greedily, for pounds. The village dogs had a feast-day.

## SERVES 4

*350g (12oz) kefalotiri or other hard cheese*
*flour, for coating*
*1 tsp dried thyme*
*black pepper*
*4 tbsp olive oil*
*lemon wedges, to serve*

Cut the cheese into eight thick slices. Season the flour with the thyme and pepper and toss the cheese slices until they are evenly coated.

Heat the oil in a large frying-pan and, when it is really hot, add the cheese. Fry it for 2 minutes on each side until it is golden brown on the outside and melting within.

Serve on – preferably – hot plates, with the lemon wedges and plenty of country bread.

---

## SARDINE OMELETTE

*Omeleta me sarthelles*

Even when there isn't a taverna in sight and the only open door belongs to a *kafenion*, I never give up hope of acquiring a simple meal. A kindly proprietor will usually unearth a piece of bread, a few tomatoes and a tin of fish.

On Lesbos, miles from anywhere, we were luckier still. Our café host produced some left-over fried sardines, a few eggs and a blackened pan. As he removed the coffee pot from the tiny gas burner he told us that this omelette is a local speciality.

## SERVES 2

*4 eggs*
*salt and black pepper*
*2 tbsp chopped parsley*
*2 tbsp olive oil*
*225g (8oz) cooked sardines, skinned, boned and*
*mashed, or use canned ones, well drained*
*1 tsp lemon juice*

Beat the eggs with 4 tbsp water, season them with salt and pepper and stir in 1 tbsp parsley.

Heat the oil in a large omelette pan, add the mashed sardines, sprinkle with the lemon juice and cook over medium heat for 2 minutes. Pour on the egg mixture, cover the pan with a lid or plate and cook for about 4–5 minutes, until the omelette is just set on top.

Slide it on to a large plate, place the pan over it and invert, to return the omelette upside-down to the pan. Cook for a further 2–3 minutes until the base is light brown. Do not overcook: omelettes all too soon become tough and leathery.

Turn the omelette on to a heated serving plate – something of a luxury in a *kafenion* – and sprinkle it with the remaining parsley. Cut it in wedges to serve.

---

## Thyme

The lingering scent of wild thyme and the hazy drift of its mass of blue-mauve flowers are high among the joys of exploring rural Greece. After an arduous climb up a rocky goat track, there is something uniquely refreshing about collapsing in a heap beside a tufty hummock of this most aromatic of hardy plants.

The species most often encountered in Greece and the one thought to have been grown by the ancients is *T. capitatus*, which has, perhaps, the most powerful scent of all. An extract of the oil, thymol, has long been valued for its antiseptic qualities, and the herb was also used in the treatment of respiratory and digestive ailments.

Turning to matters culinary, I don't know of any herb that does more to enhance a dish of meat, poultry or fish for grilling or roasting, or is more versatile in aromatic infusions. Sprinkle the fresh or dried leaves – flowers, too, if you can gather them – over steak and cuts of baby lamb or goat before barbecuing, over lamb or pork chops before frying, and over chicken before roasting. Combine the herb with rice, nuts and other ingredients to 'lift' a poultry stuffing, and with tomatoes and other flavouring vegetables when baking fish. Infuse sprigs of thyme in olive oil and vinegar for use in subtle salad dressings, in sauces and casseroles, and tuck them into jars of pickled fish and vegetables.

## FRIED SQUID WITH GARLIC SAUCE

*Kalamarakia tiganita me skorthalia*

Chios is *the* island producer of mastic, the curious crystalline substance that oozes out of the lentisk tree and finds its way, via the endeavours of some two dozen 'mastic villages', into chewing gum, liqueur and a jelly-like jam. But my over-riding Chian memory is not of enjoying many a spoonful of this *ypovrychion* ('submarine') in a glass of water but of something quite different – a harbour-side taverna sizzling with frying squid and reeking of garlic.

### SERVES 6

*1kg (2¼lb) squid (kalamares), cleaned, washed
and thoroughly dried
60g (2 ½ oz) flour
salt and black pepper
2 tsp dried oregano
oil, for deep or shallow frying*

*SAUCE
450g (1lb) potatoes, peeled
salt
8 cloves garlic, crushed
350ml (12fl oz) olive oil
juice of 2 lemons
black pepper*

First make the garlic sauce, an alternative to the *skorthalia* made with bread that is given on page 45. Boil the potatoes in salted water until they are soft, then strain and mash them. There is nothing quite like the traditional stone pestle and mortar for reducing them to the smooth, thick paste that forms the basis of this sauce. A blender might be thought to be the modern equivalent, but in this case it isn't. It produces a paste that is far too slack and runny to take up the oil.

Beat in the crushed garlic, then gradually pour on the oil and lemon juice, a few drops at a time, beating constantly. Season the sauce with salt and pepper, cover the bowl and set it aside for at least 1 hour for the flavours to blend.

Cut the squid into manageable pieces and toss them in the flour seasoned with salt, pepper and oregano.

Heat the oil for frying by whichever method you choose. Deep fry the squid in several batches for about 3 minutes, until each piece is light golden brown, or shallow fry for 2–3 minutes on each side, turning carefully so that the pieces crisp and brown evenly.

Lift out the pieces of squid with a draining spoon and toss them on kitchen paper to remove excess oil. Serve hot or warm, with the garlic sauce and plenty of bread.

*Above: Pots of basil and strings of tomatoes, the perfect combination, on Chios. Below: Goats in a pastoral setting promote thoughts of farm-made yoghurt. Right: Strips of onions dry in almost-too-perfect conditions on Chios.*

## STEAK WITH THYME

*Fileto me thimari*

We had veered way off course on Lesbos, setting off on a wild-goose chase in search of the Roman aqueduct which, I hate to admit, we never did find. But all was not quite lost. We came across a meadow painted purple with wild thyme flowers and filled a paper bag to take home – the perfect holiday gift for cookery-keen friends. It's a flavour that has a special affinity with meat and poultry of all kinds.

### SERVES 4

about 1kg (2¼lb) rump steak
40g (1½oz) butter, melted
black pepper
2 tbsp lemon juice
1–2 tbsp dried thyme flowers or, if not available,
use the dried leaves
lemon wedges, to serve

### THYME BUTTER
100g (4oz) unsalted butter, softened
2 cloves garlic, crushed
2 tsp lemon juice
1 tbsp fresh thyme leaves
black pepper

Begin by making the savoury butter, which you can do several days in advance. Beat the butter well. Beat in the garlic, lemon juice and fresh thyme and season well with pepper. Shape the butter into a roll, wrap it in foil and chill in the refrigerator.

Cut the steak into four pieces. Brush the meat on both sides with the melted butter, season with pepper and sprinkle on the lemon juice. Sprinkle half the thyme evenly on to one side of the steaks.

Grill the meat under high heat for 3–4 minutes. Turn the meat, baste with any pan juices and sprinkle with the remaining thyme. Grill for a further 3–4 minutes or until the steak is as rare or as well done as you like it. The exact time required will depend, of course, to a large extent on the thickness of the meat.

Serve the steaks with the lemon wedges and topped by pats of the herb butter.

A chilled green salad tossed with a sprinkling of fresh thyme goes especially well.

## FISH MAYONNAISE

*Psari me mayioneza*

Lemnos has so much more to offer than the usual leisure-seekers' trio of joyful requirements, sun, sea and sand. The island has been inhabited since Neolithic times, and its ancient city sites pull the visitor like magnets, yielding unforgettable glimpses of times long past.

The island's restaurants and hotels offer more than the 'average' repertoire of local dishes, too, including this as-elaborate-as-you-care-to-make-it summer fish dish.

### SERVES 4

1kg (2¼lb) white fish fillets
1 medium onion, sliced
1 carrot, quartered
2 stalks celery, sliced
2 bay leaves
a few stalks parsley
2 tbsp lemon juice
salt
1 tsp black peppercorns
vegetables for decoration (see method)

### MAYONNAISE
2 egg yolks
2 tbsp lemon juice
300ml (½ pint) olive oil
salt and black pepper
2 tsp grated lemon rind

Put the fish into a large pan with the onion, carrot, celery and herbs and pour on just enough water to cover the fish. Add the lemon juice, salt and peppercorns and bring the water slowly to the boil. Cover the pan and simmer for 10 minutes. Leave the fish to cool in the liquid, then carefully lift it out and dry it thoroughly on kitchen paper. (You can use the liquid as a basis for fish soup or a sauce.) Arrange the fish on a serving dish and set it aside.

To make the mayonnaise, beat the egg yolks with 1 tsp of the lemon juice until they thicken slightly. Add the oil a few drops at a time, then a little more lemon juice, more oil and so on. Once the sauce becomes thick and creamy you can quicken the pace and add the oil in a steady stream, still beating all the time. Season the sauce with salt and pepper and beat in the lemon rind. Taste and adjust the seasoning if necessary.

Spread the sauce over the fish to give a thick, even coating – the exact amount you need will depend on the actual surface area to be covered.

Now your artistic talents can have free rein.

Decorate the mayonnaise with capers, sliced cucumber, strips of red, green and yellow pepper, prawns – whatever comes to hand and to mind.

Serve the fish with a green salad and another salad of tiny new potatoes, tossed, while they are still hot, in a vinaigrette dressing.

# Olive Oil

Brushed on to the shimmering scales of fish before grilling; drizzled over slices of feta cheese and chunks of country bread to enhance a work-day snack; heated in a blackened iron pan until it is smoke-hazy to sear quick-cooking cuts of meat; poured in a steady stream over crisp and colourful salad vegetables to give the characteristic flavour to *horiatikisalata* (Greek country salad); combined with robust local wine and spices as a preserving medium for fish and vegetables (octopus and globe artichokes, for example); gently heated to get casserole vegetables off to a tender and tasty start; or sprinkled on to the surface of chick-pea purée until it glistens … where would Greek cuisine be without the benefit of olive oil?

The silver-green and almost iridescent trees that cover so much of the countryside – one estimate puts the number at 7 million trees on Corfu alone – have their roots firmly planted in Greek history and culture, and there is evidence that olive oil has sustained the national diet since Neolithic and Minoan times.

In an ideal world, the trees would have all the water they need – which is a considerable amount; but where efficient irrigation is not possible or practicable, the crop suffers, and trees bear fruit only in alternate years. A high proportion of the olives grown in Greece – as much as 98 per cent in some regions – is destined for the production of olive oil either, increasingly, in modern factories or in locally run co-operative units set up in the midst of an olive grove. The fruit has a very high oil yield, which can vary between 75 and 82 per cent, and the fruit from a

single well-established tree can yield as much as 100 litres (22 gallons) of oil.

The finest quality oil, known as 'extra virgin' or, more helpfully, 'extra virgin unrefined', is made simply by crushing fresh, cold, first-grade olives; no heating or other processing is involved. The oil should be a pale, clear yellow and completely odourless. The product described as 'pure olive oil' may have been pressed from the pulp and kernals of second-grade fruit, and the third quality, which usually has a greenish colour and a pronounced odour, is made from secondary pressings under heat.

Whenever the character of the oil is a significant feature of a dish, as it is in salads, sauces, dressings and garnishes, it is well worth the extra cost involved in using the finest grade you can buy.

Olive oil, like all other fats, has recently come under intense scrutiny by the health-conscious among us. The breakdown of fatty acids – approximately 12 per cent polyunsaturates, 16 per cent saturated fatty acids and 72 per cent monounsaturates – makes olive oil somewhat neutral in health terms. It has neither the high level of saturated fat found in solid fats such as butter, nor the supposed cholesterol-lowering properties of other vegetable oils such as sunflower and safflower, which are much higher in polyunsaturates. But when a Greek friend hands you a bottle of oil pressed from the finest olives his village can grow, such considerations do not spring immediately to mind.

# LEMNOS VEAL

*Mosharaki Limnou*

With all that delectable yoghurt maturing in every farmhouse kitchen, to say nothing of the excellent brands you can buy in the cafés and shops, I have always been rather surprised that Greek culinary tradition does not draw on it more generously as an ingredient. So I was delighted, in an inland taverna on Lemnos, to be served this rich and creamy veal dish.

### SERVES 4

*4 tbsp olive oil*
*1 medium onion, finely chopped*
*2 cloves garlic, crushed*
*450g (1lb) lean veal, minced*
*75g (3oz) breadcrumbs*
*1 tbsp chopped coriander or parsley*
*salt and black pepper*
*flour, for dusting*
*50g (2oz) butter*

### SAUCE

*1 tbsp plain flour*
*200ml (6fl oz) chicken stock*
*salt and black pepper*
*150ml (1/4 pint) Greek yoghurt*
*1 tbsp chopped coriander or parsley*

Heat 2 tbsp oil in a large frying-pan and fry the onion over medium heat until it is transparent. Add the crushed garlic and fry for 1 minute more.

Turn the onion mixture into a bowl and add the veal. Mash it well with a wooden spoon to make a sticky paste. Stir in the breadcrumbs and chopped herb, season with salt and pepper and mix thoroughly.

Flour your hands and shape the meat mixture into rounds somewhat smaller than golf balls. Roll each one in flour until it is well coated.

Heat the remaining oil and the butter in the pan and fry the meat balls until they are lightly coloured on all sides. This will take 7–8 minutes.

Lift out the meat balls with a draining spoon and set them aside. Stir in the flour and, when it has formed a roux, gradually pour on the stock, stirring

*Pages 86–7: Lemnos Veal.*

constantly. Season the sauce with salt and pepper, return the meat balls to the pan and slowly bring the sauce to the boil. Cover the pan and simmer over low heat for 30 minutes, turning the meat once or twice.

Stir in the yoghurt and reheat the sauce gently, without allowing it to come to the boil. Taste the sauce and adjust the seasoning if necessary. Sprinkle with the chopped herb before serving.

Buttered noodles tossed with plenty of fresh herbs make a lovely accompaniment.

———————

# BEEF WITH COURGETTES

*Moshari me kolokithakia*

My visit to Samos nearly changed my life. And then it didn't. I was telling a weather-beaten old goatherd how lucky he was to have a never-ending supply of fresh, creamy yoghurt.

'Well,' he said, 'you could have the same where you live, if you don't mind the goats eating all your vegetables and flowers, and if you're prepared to get up at four in the morning to milk them.' I wasn't, quite, so I'm grateful that we can now buy such good brands of Greek yoghurt in our local shops.

### SERVES 4–6

*1kg (2 1/4 lb) lean beef, trimmed of excess fat, cubed*
*3 tbsp olive oil*
*2 medium onions, chopped*
*2 stalks celery, thinly sliced*
*2 cloves garlic, finely chopped*
*3 tbsp tomato purée*
*salt and black pepper*
*1 tsp ground cumin*
*450g (1lb) courgettes, trimmed and sliced*
*150ml (1/4 pint) Greek yoghurt*

Dry the meat cubes on kitchen paper. Heat the oil in a large pan and fry the meat in one or two batches over medium heat, turning them over and over until they are evenly coloured. Lift out the meat with a draining spoon and set it aside.

Fry the onion and celery in the pan for about 3 minutes, then stir in the garlic and cook for 1–2 minutes more. Stir in the tomato purée, return the meat to the pan and pour on 600ml (1 pint) water. Season with salt and pepper and the ground cumin and stir well. Bring to the boil, cover the pan and simmer for 1½ hours. Add the courgettes and simmer for 20–25 minutes, until the meat and courgettes are tender. Taste the sauce and adjust the seasoning if necessary. If it is a little too runny, increase the heat and cook, uncovered, to evaporate some of the liquid. Just before serving, stir in the yoghurt and then reheat the sauce without allowing it to boil.

---

# LAMB AND MACARONI PIE

*Pastitsio*

The Greeks don't have the same derogatory 'yesterday's mashed potatoes' attitude as we do to cold food. And indeed, many dishes that make their first appearance straight from the oven really are just as appetizing when served cold, even though it may be the second time around. This pasta pie is a case in point.

One idyllic spring day, a friend took a huge round, oozing, bubbly-brown tray of it on a picnic to a deserted cove on the island of Thassos. Both the cold pie and the golden-blue setting were pure delight.

### SERVES 4–6

*4 tbsp olive oil*
*1 medium onion, chopped*
*2 cloves garlic, crushed*
*450g (1lb) lean lamb, minced*
*2 medium carrots, grated*
*450g (1lb) canned tomatoes, chopped*
*100ml (4fl oz) white wine*
*4 tbsp chopped coriander or parsley*
*salt and black pepper*
*225g (8oz) short-cut macaroni*
*50g (2oz) butter*
*4 tbsp kefalotiri or other hard cheese, grated*

### TOPPING
*300ml (½ pint) Greek yoghurt*
*2 eggs*
*salt and black pepper*
*grated nutmeg*
*4 tbsp kefalotiri or other hard cheese, grated*

Heat the oil in a frying-pan and fry the onion over medium heat until it is transparent. Add the garlic and fry for 1 minute more. Add the minced lamb and cook, stirring at intervals, until it is evenly light brown. Add the carrot, tomatoes, wine and 2 tbsp of the chopped herb and season with salt and pepper. Cook the meat mixture for about 15 minutes or until the excess liquid has evaporated or been absorbed. It should then be the consistency of a thick paste.

Meanwhile, cook the macaroni in a large pan of boiling, salted water until it is just tender. Tip it into a colander, bounce it up and down to drain it well and tip it into a bowl. Stir in the butter, the remaining chopped herb and the grated cheese and season with salt and pepper.

To make the topping, beat together the yoghurt and eggs and season the mixture with salt, pepper and a few gratings of nutmeg.

Grease a large baking tin (I use one 25 x 18 x 7·5cm (10 x 7 x 3in). Spread half the macaroni over the base, cover it with the meat mixture, and then with the remaining macaroni. Pour the yoghurt topping evenly over the surface and sprinkle on the cheese.

Bake in the oven at 190°C (375°F/Gas 5) for 25–30 minutes, until the top is golden brown and bubbling. Serve hot or cold.

## Stabilizing Yoghurt

If you add cold yoghurt to a hot soup or casserole, it will almost certainly separate. To avoid this happening, you can stabilize a batch of yoghurt every now and then, and keep it for cooking.

To stabilize 1 litre (1¾ pints) of yoghurt, use one lightly whisked egg white or 15ml (1 tablespoon) of cornflour mixed to a smooth paste with a little water or milk. Bring the yoghurt and the stabilizer slowly to the boil, stirring gently and in only one direction all the time. Once the yoghurt reaches boiling point, turn the heat to its lowest setting, put the pan on a heat diffuser if you have one, and leave it, uncovered, for 10 minutes. Remove the pan from the heat, allow the yoghurt to cool, then store it in a covered container in the refrigerator for up to two weeks.

*Left: Well wooded and intensely fertile, Samos is one of the few truly 'green' islands. Top: A door-to-door salesman – and his donkey – brighten a village roadway.*
*Above: Thyme flowers, the most evocative of take-home presents, are perfect sprinkled on meats for roasting and grilling.*

# CHESTNUT MOUNTAIN

*Glykisma me kastana*

Thassos is an intensely, densely green island – except, that is, in spring, when the chestnuts are in blossom and the orchards are dappled romantically with the confetti-like pink and white petals that promise such a bountiful harvest of pomegranates and peaches, plums and pears.

Accordingly, sweets and desserts have a higher than usual profile in the local tradition. This chestnut dessert, reminiscent of the Italian *mont blanc*, was offered to us in an island home but proved to be sadly elusive in confectioners' shops.

## SERVES 4

*1kg (2¼lb) chestnuts*
*salt*
*900ml (1½ pints) milk*
*50g (2oz) sugar*
*4 tbsp honey*
*1 tsp vanilla essence*
*75g (3oz) grated chocolate*
*5 tbsp brandy*
*Greek yoghurt, to serve*
*grated chocolate, to decorate (optional)*

Slit the chestnuts and cook them in a pan of boiling, salted water for 20–25 minutes. Drain them, allow them to cool until you can handle them, then peel off the skins and the brown inner skins.

Halve the chestnuts and place them in a saucepan with the milk, sugar, honey and vanilla essence. Cook them over low heat for 40–45 minutes until the chestnuts are soft and have absorbed the milk. Purée them in a blender or food processor, rub them through a coarse sieve or press them through a food mill.

Return the chestnut purée to the pan, add the grated chocolate and brandy and stir until the mixture forms a thick paste.

Pile the dessert into individual serving dishes and top with swirls of yoghurt. Decorate each dish with grated chocolate if you wish.

Sometimes, for a quick and totally unauthentic version of this dessert, I beat a tin of unsweetened chestnut purée until it is soft, then stir in the honey, chocolate and brandy, melted and heated together.

# ALMOND PEARS

*Amigthalota*

Nothing we had read about Ikaria – the ruins of the ancient city of Dionysias, the chain of tiny villages strung hospitably up the mountain slopes, the balconies burgeoning with flowers and the gardens blossoming with fruit and nut trees – had prepared us for the joyful, tranquil beauty of the island. And yet, the first time, we went there by mistake, having jostled on to the wrong boat. It was a happy accident.

## MAKES 12

*450g (1lb) blanched almonds*
*175g (6oz) caster sugar*
*75g (3oz) fine semolina*
*3 egg whites*
*2 tbsp orange-flower water, plus extra for brushing*
*12 cloves*
*icing sugar, for dusting*

Grind the almonds in a blender or food processor and turn them into a bowl. Stir in the sugar, semolina, egg whites and orange-flower water and mix to a smooth, stiff paste. If the paste is too slack or too sticky to shape – and that will depend on the size of the egg whites you have used– stir in a little more semolina.

Shape the almond paste into 12 pear shapes – or you could cheat and make apples instead – and insert a clove in the top of each.

Arrange the sweets on a greased baking sheet and bake them in the oven at 180°C (350°F/Gas 4) for 15–20 minutes until they are crisp on the outside and lightly coloured. Set aside to cool.

Brush the cooled pears with orange-flower water and carefully dip them in icing sugar to coat. Leave them to set for a few minutes, then dust them with sugar again.

Serve the pears as a sweetmeat with Greek coffee and iced water.

# SESAME AND HONEY TOFFEE

## *Pasteli*

Much as I love the sight and sound of multi-hued fishing boats rising and falling against a harbour wall, I can't wait to explore the way-off-the-beaten-track villages at the heart of an island.

On Lemnos this proved to be a particularly rewarding pastime, as one after another Turkish-style village rises from the almost treeless landscape. In one such village we were presented with this charming token of welcome, a chewy toffee, which was offered, paper-wrapped, with a glass of ice-cold water and the request to please come by again.

### MAKES ABOUT 750g (1½lb)

*450g (1lb) honey*
*100g (4oz) sugar*
*225g (8oz) sesame seeds*

If you happen to have Lemnian honey, so much the better, for the island is renowned for the quality and aroma of its local product.

Pour the honey into a small, heavy, thick-bottomed pan – a cast-iron one is ideal – and stir in the sugar and sesame seeds. Cook over medium heat for about 15 minutes, stirring occasionally, until the honey deepens in colour. Have ready a cup with a little cold water. Drop in about 1 tsp of the honey mixture. If it is ready, it should immediately form into a compact ball that feels resistant to the fingers when pressed. If you have a sugar thermometer, the mixture should reach 120–130°C (248–266°F).

When it is ready, pour the mixture into a lightly oiled tin such as a Swiss roll tin and leave it to set. Mark it in squares as soon as it starts to harden, to make it easier to break neatly.

Cut the toffee into squares. Wrap each one in greaseproof paper if you wish and store it in an airtight tin. It would keep indefinitely if it weren't so irresistible.

# Greek Coffee

Greek coffee is, in truth, Turkish coffee – it is said to have been introduced into Europe via Turkey in the sixteenth century – but it is not tactful to describe it as such when you are on Greek soil.

Making coffee is both a ritual and a matter of national pride, and every detail of the procedure is given the closest attention. Witness the glow of pleasure on the face of a villager who offers you a cup of coffee in his garden, or the proprietor of the most modest *kafenion* as he carries the minute cup and its accompanying glass of water on a battered aluminium tray. That coffee represents the very essence of Greek hospitality.

To make Greek coffee for yourself, you can buy very finely ground powder or, for a more authentic result, grind beans almost to a dust in one of those tall, cylindrical and highly decorative Balkan coffee grinders. It is possible to make the coffee in a small saucepan, but we'll forget that and opt for a *briki*, the traditional long-handled metal pot, rather like a jug, with a pouring lip. You can buy them very cheaply in various sizes in general stores.

Measure the water in the coffee cups, pour just the right amount into the pot and bring it to the boil. Add about 10ml (a heaped teaspoonful) of coffee for each cup, let it settle on the top and then add sugar to taste. (If someone wants sweet coffee and someone else wants it without sugar, you will have to make it separately.) Bring the water to the boil again, still without stirring, then remove the pot from the heat to let the froth subside. Repeat this process once more, then bring the coffee back to the boil for the final time, stir it to distribute the grounds evenly, and pour it into the cups immediately, before they settle. Serve a glass of chilled water with each cup. And remember that the leisurely enjoyment of Greek coffee is the best part of the ritual.

# CHAPTER 6

# Evia and the Sporades

Evia, which is, after Crete, the second largest Greek island, has everything going for it – and not a lot of people who know that. It shimmers with the frosty greenness of olives, poplars and pines; it is dappled from one season to another with an artist's palette of pink Judas-tree blossom, mallow, tree heather and oleander, and it groans under the weight, so to speak, of grapes, figs, pomegranates, walnuts and chestnuts.

Two of these crops come together in a tasty walnut and grape preserve, known as *sesfikia*. Your first glimpse of it might be as long, thin, honey-coloured strings that look like sausages, hanging from tree branches in village gardens – in Ohthonia, for example – or in small general stores. The recipe, a masterpiece of sensible thrift, involves boiling up the must left over after wine-making until it thickens, dipping shelled walnuts to coat them roundly and hanging them on strings to dry in the sun. These fresh nuts with a soft, chewy coating are then put aside to be enjoyed as a Christmas sweetmeat. But for those who can't wait that long, the paste can be served warm, straight out of the cauldron, as a dessert, sprinkled with chopped walnuts – *karithia*.

The little port of Paralia Kimi is the stepping-stone to Skyros, the closest of the Sporades islands. It has a sufficiency of small waterside tavernas, the kind where you needn't be afraid to ask for your favourite dish to be cooked, another day. The beach is long, sandy and wild, shaded by pampas grass and punctuated by blue-domed fishermen's chapels. And, until the grape harvest, it is considered the natural place to store row after row of wine barrels.

Across the water, on Skopelos, housewives cling to their culinary heritage and make a speciality of sweet almond cakes, walnut pies and fruit preserves of all kinds. Alonissos, which greets the visitor with a drift of sage, thyme and oregano, has an excellent local sour cheese known as *xynogalo* and, in the autumn, a mixed bag of game. Cooks on Skiathos specialize in rissoles of various kinds, made from cods' roe (see page 96), courgettes,

*Opposite: Tending the goats way off the beaten track on Evia.
Below: A wayside chapel decorated with a* stefani, *a floral ring made in celebration of May Day.*

minced meat and even sea anemones, while on Skyros the specialities range from custard pies (see page 104) to dried bean soup flavoured with wild fennel and lemon juice.

Our introduction to Skyros was unconventional. Two middle-aged sisters approached us as we left the bus in the old town of Hora and announced that, as my husband, Douglas, had an honest face, we would be permitted to rent their late parents' house. Which we joyfully did. Kept almost as a shrine to the departed couple, it was a time capsule of Skyrian culture, with three carved wooden beds around the living room walls, a huge tapestry-covered table in the centre and a beehive oven in the corner. In true Skyrian style, shelves were closely packed with expensive blue and white china

and the walls were hung with dozens of gleaming copper pans. The practicalities were not overlooked – there was a shallow granite sink and a tiny portable gas burner in an alcove, and a small cubicle out in the street.

It didn't take long for word to get around that I was interested in cooking, and every day I was invited into one after another kitchen, well before breakfast, to help make a stuffing for a chicken, the filling for a pie, or garlic sauce to serve with fish. Having watched the coral sun rise so many times over the neighbourhood chapel as I chopped and pounded and stirred, I began to realize that this time, long before the heat of the day takes over, really is the best for creative cooking. I only wish I could say that I had kept it up!

---

## PICKLED OCTOPUS

### *Htapothi toursi*

Amarinthos on Evia wouldn't be everyone's idea of a picture-postcard town or village, but it has one greatly redeeming feature – several, in fact. The main, coast-hugging road is teeming with lively fish tavernas and with the most artistic still-life displays of gleaming, glistening, caught-this-morning fish spotlighted on roadside stalls. And every family matriarch, or *yia-yia*, seems to do a good line in pickled octopus, which is served with ouzo as an appetizer.

### SERVES 8

*1kg (2¼lb) young octopus*
*about 150ml (¼ pint) olive oil*
*about 150ml (¼ pint) red wine vinegar*
*4 cloves garlic, crushed*
*salt and black pepper*
*4–6 stalks thyme or 1 tsp dried thyme*
*lemon wedges, to serve*

Prepare and wash the octopus as described on page 13. Place the head and tentacles in a pan with 6–8 tbsp water, cover and simmer for 1–1¼ hours until

it is tender. Test it with a skewer. Drain off any remaining liquid and set aside to cool.

Cut the flesh into 12mm (½in) strips and pack them loosely into a screw-topped jar. Mix enough oil and vinegar to fill the jar – the exact amount will depend on the relative volumes of the seafood and the container – stir in the garlic and season with salt and pepper. If you are using dried thyme, mix it with the liquid at this stage. Pour it over the octopus, making sure that every last piece is completely immersed. If you are using thyme stalks, push them into the jar.

Cover the jar and set it aside for at least 4–5 days before using.

To serve, drain the octopus and serve it on small individual plates or saucers with the lemon wedges.

Cubes of at least one-day-old bread, speared on cocktail sticks, are the usual accompaniment.

---

## CODS' ROE RISSOLES

### *Taramokeftethes*

Don't shoot the cookery writer who says that *taramokeftethes* are one of the culinary delights of Skiathos if you get there and don't find them on a single taverna menu. Sadly, that only illustrates the gulf that can exist these days between regional home cooking and the more generalized commercial fare on offer.

If you get to know a taverna proprietor, perhaps you could talk him into making them for you, or give yourself a taste of the Sporades and cook them back home.

### SERVES 4

*4 slices white bread, crusts removed*
*3 tbsp olive oil, plus more for shallow frying*
*2 medium onions, sliced*
*225g (8oz) smoked cods' roe, skinned*
*25g (1oz) fine semolina*
*2 tbsp lemon juice*
*6 tbsp chopped coriander or parsley*
*black pepper*
*flour, for coating*
*lemon wedges, to serve*

Soak the bread in water for about 15 minutes, then remove it and squeeze it dry. Heat the oil in a small pan and fry the onion over medium heat until it just begins to colour.

Put the cods' roe, crumbled bread and onion into a blender or food processor and blend only until it makes a coarse paste. You're not into making a smooth purée.

Scrape the mixture into a bowl and stir in the semolina, lemon juice and chopped herb. Season with pepper and mix well.

Flour your hands, shape the mixture into fat sausages and dust them with flour.

Heat the oil for shallow frying in a large frying-pan over medium heat and fry the 'sausages' for 7–8 minutes, turning them frequently so that they brown evenly on all sides.

Roll them on kitchen paper to dry them and serve hot, although they are remarkably good cold. Serve with lemon wedges and, if you like, boiled potatoes and a green vegetable.

## Ouzo

Ask many a Graecophile – my husband, for example – to muse on his favourite form of relaxation on a Greek island and there he will be, transported in his mind's eye to a busy harbourside, with a glass of milky-white ouzo on the table before him, and most importantly, a plate of charcoal-blackened octopus as *mezethakia* to accompany it.

With its strong, some say overpowering flavour of aniseed, ouzo isn't everyone's ideal aperitif, but in the right place, at the right time and, I have to say, in moderation, it is a vital part of the ambience that is Greece (although ouzo is, in fact, also made in most Middle Eastern countries).

The spirit is distilled from grapes and is usually a by-product of the wine-making process. Some types are made by adding aniseed and other herbs to spirit that has been distilled twice – a refinement, this – and some Greek brands are flavoured with mastic, which gives more than a hint of liquorice.

Clear and colourless, the spirit is usually

served in a tall, narrow straight-sided glass, and it is always accompanied by a glass of chilled water. Although the sturdiest of islanders may frown on the custom and the resultant dilution of the spirit, the idea is to pour a little of the water on to the ouzo, which will turn cloudy. Bought locally, ouzo is a relatively inexpensive drink.

Ouzo is never offered without some kind of food, however simple. It may be gnarled and knobbly chunks of octopus, tiny vine leaf parcels, cubes of day-old bread with slices of local cheese and cucumber, or simply a bowl of peanuts or olives. Indeed, the *mezethakia* can be such an important part of the leisurely pre-prandial ritual that many devotees select an *ouzaria* (specialist bar) or a *kafenion* for the quality and variety of the accompanying appetizers. And for the view, of course.

# SALT COD WITH COURGETTES

*Bakalarios me kolokithakia*

For several weeks before Easter, wooden boxes of leathery looking salt cod are a familiar sight in general stores on the islands, the prime ingredient of a traditional Lenten dish.

It's amazing what a good long soaking in cool, clear water can do – and how delicious and appetizing this preserved fish becomes when it's cooked with a medley of fresh and colourful vegetables.

### SERVES 4–6

750g (1$^1$/2lb) dried salt cod
8 tbsp olive oil
1 green pepper, cored, seeded and cut into rings
2 medium onions, sliced
6 cloves garlic, chopped
450g (1lb) tomatoes, skinned and chopped
6 tbsp red wine
1 tsp sugar
2 tbsp lemon juice
black pepper
225g (8oz) courgettes, thinly sliced
2 tbsp chopped coriander or parsley
lemon wedges, to serve

### SALAD
$^1$/2 small firm lettuce, sliced
$^1$/2 cucumber, sliced and quartered
6 spring onions, trimmed and sliced
3 tbsp chopped coriander or parsley
5 tbsp olive oil
2 tbsp red wine vinegar
salt and black pepper

Soak the cod in a bowl of cold water for about 24 hours, changing the water once or twice. Skin and bone the fish and cut the flesh into pieces.

Heat 6 tbsp of the oil in a frying-pan. Fry the pepper rings over medium heat for 1 minute on each side, lift them out with a draining spoon and set them aside.

Fry the fish for 3 minutes on each side, then lift it out with a draining spoon.

Add the remaining 2 tbsp oil and fry the onions until they are transparent. Add the garlic and fry for 1 minute more. Add the tomatoes, wine and sugar, stir well and bring to the boil. Cover and simmer the sauce for 10 minutes. Stir in the lemon juice, season with pepper and return the fish to the pan. Spoon the sauce over it, cover the pan and simmer very slowly for 45 minutes. If the sauce shows signs of drying out in this time, add a little water.

Add the courgettes, cover the pan and simmer for a further 15 minutes. Stir in 1 tbsp of the chopped herb. Taste the sauce and adjust the seasoning if necessary. Arrange the pepper rings on

top and allow them to heat through. Sprinkle on the remaining coriander or parsley and garnish the dish with lemon wedges.

To make the salad, toss together the lettuce, cucumber, spring onions and chopped herb. Mix the oil and vinegar, season the dressing with salt and pepper and pour it over the salad. Toss well to coat the salad in the dressing. For a touch of authenticity, garnish the salad, if possible, with a courgette flower.

*Salt Cod with Courgettes, a Lenten dish.*

99

# EEL SOUP

## *Heli soupa*

For many a holiday-maker, even self-confessed Graecophiles, Evia offers a new voyage of discovery. Well, not much of a voyage, actually, since this green and fertile only-just-an-island stands a mere 88km (55 miles) from the centre of Athens and is connected to the mainland by a drawbridge.

But with many a dazzling Byzantine church, a once-daunting Venetian fortress and a remote, prehistoric city site to its credit, it has more than its fair share of exploration potential. Fish and game are the main menu-makers, with eels being a local delicacy.

### SERVES 4–6

*8 tbsp olive oil*
*2 medium onions, sliced*
*6 stalks celery, thickly sliced*
*2 cloves garlic, finely chopped*
*1kg (2¼lb) eel, skinned and cut into 4cm (1½in)*
*pieces*
*1·75 litres (3 pints) fish stock (see page 17) or*
*water*
*2 bay leaves*
*salt and black pepper*
*75g (3oz) long-grain rice, washed and drained*
*2 eggs*
*juice of 2 lemons*
*2 tsp cornflour*
*2 tbsp chopped parsley*

Heat 4 tbsp of the oil in a large pan and fry the onions and celery over medium heat for 3–4 minutes. Add the garlic and fry for 1–2 minutes more. Add the pieces of eel, pour on the stock or water, add the bay leaves and season with salt and pepper. Bring to the boil, cover the pan and simmer for 45 minutes.

Add the rice, return the soup to the boil, cover and simmer for a further 12–15 minutes until the rice is cooked.

If you wish, you can remove the eel from the soup at this stage, cut the flesh away from the bones and return it to the pan.

Beat together the eggs and lemon juice. Mix the cornflour to a smooth paste with 2 tbsp water and combine the two. Stir in a little of the hot soup, then pour the mixture into the pan. Heat gently, without boiling, until the soup starts to thicken. Taste and adjust the seasoning if necessary. Sprinkle the remaining olive oil on the soup just before serving. Up to this point, the soup is somewhat lacking in colour – scatter on the chopped parsley to take care of that.

---

# FRIED FISH WITH TOMATO SAUCE

## *Psaria tiganita me saltsa domatas*

What's in a name? So much more than is evident from many a recipe description, that's for sure. Here is a dish that is the very essence of island culinary tradition among the fisherfolk of Alonissos. It is at its best, I have to say, when prepared with today's catch and cooked over a gas burner in the street outside a harbourside cottage.

### SERVES 4

*4 medium mackerel, cleaned, washed and dried*
*salt and black pepper*
*juice of 2 lemons*
*4 tbsp flour*
*2 tsp dried oregano*
*6 tbsp olive oil*
*2 medium onions, sliced*
*2 cloves garlic, finely chopped*
*2 large tomatoes, skinned and chopped*
*2 tbsp tomato purée*
*5 tbsp red wine vinegar*
*4–5 stalks parsley*
*2 tbsp chopped celery leaves*

Make three slashes on each side of each of the fish. Season the fish inside and out with salt and pepper and place them in a shallow dish. Pour over the lemon juice and set aside to marinate for at least 2 hours, turning the fish once.

Season the flour with salt, pepper and the oregano and toss the fish to coat it thoroughly. Heat the oil in a large pan and fry the fish over medium heat for 4–5 minutes on each side. Lift the fish out and set them aside.

Fry the onions until they just begin to colour. Add the garlic and fry for 1–2 minutes more. Stir in the tomatoes, tomato purée and vinegar and mix well. Pour on 150ml (¼ pint) water, add the parsley and celery leaves and bring to the boil. Cover the pan and simmer for 15–20 minutes until the sauce has thickened. Place the fish in the sauce, spoon it over to cover them and cover the pan. Simmer for 10–15 minutes until the fish are cooked. Remove the parsley stalks. Taste the sauce and adjust the seasoning if necessary.

Serve the fish with plain boiled potatoes and the greenest of salads. I like to serve young spinach – or even dandelion leaves – drizzled with olive oil and lemon juice.

## Sweet Bay

The bay tree, with its dark green, leathery and sweetly scented leaves, has a high profile in Greek mythology; and in damp, rocky places, gullies and thickets, too. It will be recalled that Daphne, the daughter of the river god, Peneus, was saved from the unwelcome advances of Apollo when she was turned into a bay tree in his arms. The faithful and repentant Apollo made himself a crown of the leaves, and declared that the tree should be held sacred.

In ancient Greece, bay laurel wreaths were used to honour poets, military heroes and the winners of the Olympic and Pythian Games; similarly, in recent times, a crown of laurels bearing berries (*baccae*) was bestowed on newly qualified academics and doctors. The French term *baccalauréat* and the English language 'bachelor' have this derivation.

Greek cooks use bay leaves in much the same was as cooks throughout the western world – a leaf or two to flavour soups and sauces, casseroles and custards, puddings and pickles – and many have a bunch of bay leaves hanging in the kitchen to ensure they have flavour at their fingertips.

# PORK CHOPS WITH PRUNES

*Hirines brizoles me thamaskina*

You have only to stop and admire a garden on Skopelos – barely even that – and the owner will offer you the traditional expression of island hospitality, a preserved prune, a sweet almond cake and a glass of *raki*. Prunes are *the* local industry, as you will appreciate if you accept an inevitable invitation to visit the drying ovens and a packing station.

This dish, combining the sweetness of the fruit with pork, is a local speciality.

### SERVES 4

*4 pork chops, trimmed of excess fat*
*salt and black pepper*
*2 tbsp lemon juice*
*2 tbsp olive oil*
*25g (1oz) butter*
*250ml (8fl oz) red wine*
*175g (6oz) pitted prunes, pre-soaked if necessary*

This may seem an unconventional way to cook pork chops, first braising – or, to be accurate, boiling – them, then frying them to a light golden brown and, finally, braising them again. But it's very Greek and results in succulent meat. And the washer-up has no need to worry – all the cooking takes place in the one pan.

Season the chops with salt and pepper, rub them with the lemon juice and set them aside for about 30 minutes for the flavours to penetrate. Put the chops in a large frying-pan and pour on water to partly cover them. Bring it to the boil and simmer, uncovered, for about 10 minutes until the water has evaporated.

Lift out the chops, pat them dry and heat the oil and butter in the pan. Return the chops to the pan and fry them over medium heat until they are light brown on both sides. Pour on the wine, season with salt and pepper and add the prunes. Bring to the boil and simmer for 15–20 minutes until the chops are tender. Taste the sauce and adjust the seasoning if necessary.

Rice and a green salad go well with this rich and fruity dish.

# STUFFED AUBERGINES

*Melitzanes yemistes*

One of the most familiar and most versatile of Greek dishes is *yemistes* (filled vegetables), and there must be as many variations of this basic dish as there are tavernas and home cooks who prepare them.

I love to see a selection of stuffed aubergines, courgettes, tomatoes, globe artichokes and cucumbers lined up in a taverna kitchen. It's always exciting to discover just what combination of meat, herbs and spices has gone into making up that tantalizing aroma. This recipe comes from Skiathos.

### SERVES 4

*4 large aubergines*
*salt*
*4 tbsp olive oil*
*1 medium onion, chopped*
*2 red peppers, cored, seeded and chopped*
*2 cloves garlic, finely chopped*
*350g (12oz) minced lamb*
*225g (8oz) canned tomatoes, chopped*
*2 tsp dried oregano*
*2 tbsp chopped coriander or parsley*
*black pepper*
*1/2 tsp ground cumin*

### SAUCE
*300ml (1/2 pint) Greek yoghurt*
*2 eggs*
*salt and black pepper*
*50g (2oz) kefalotiri or other hard cheese, grated*

Trim the aubergines and cook them in a pan of boiling, salted water for 5–8 minutes until they begin to soften. Drain and cool the aubergines. Cut them in half lengthways and, using a teaspoon, scoop out a channel of the flesh. Be sure to leave firm 'walls'. Chop the scooped-out flesh and set it aside. Place the aubergine halves, cut sides up, in a shallow baking dish.

Heat the oil in a pan and fry the onion and pepper over medium heat for 3–4 minutes. Add the garlic and fry for 1–2 minutes more. Stir in the lamb and cook for 5–6 minutes, stirring occasionally, until the meat is evenly coloured. Stir in the chopped aubergine, the tomatoes, oregano and chopped herb and season with salt, pepper and the cumin. Cook, still over medium heat, until the mixture dries out and is like a thick paste. Spoon the meat mixture into the aubergine shells, piling it up into a neat mound.

To make the sauce, beat together the yoghurt and eggs. Season with salt and pepper and stir in half of the cheese. Pour over the aubergines and sprinkle with the remaining cheese.

Bake the dish, uncovered, in the oven at 190°C (375°F/Gas 5) for about 30 minutes until the topping is golden brown and bubbling. Serve hot.

*Above: Figs, a speciality of Evia, are one of the delights of autumn. Below: The undulating coastline of Alonissos. Right: Stuffed Aubergines.*

# CHICKEN WITH CINNAMON

*Kotopoulo me kanella*

The boat from Kimi, on Evia, arrives in the cool of the evening, and a rickety old bus rumbles and grumbles its way across Skyros to the ancient hilltop town of Hora. Then pure enchantment takes over. All at once we were too caught up in the sheer joy of the atmosphere to think about food.

When, finally, we succumbed to the friendly welcome of a pavement taverna, this was the dish we chose.

### SERVES 4

*1 oven-ready chicken, about 1·5kg (3 1/2 lb)*
*black pepper*
*2 tsp dried oregano*
*5 tbsp olive oil*
*25g (1oz) butter*
*2 medium onions, chopped*
*2 cloves garlic, finely chopped*
*450g (1lb) canned tomatoes, chopped*
*2 tbsp tomato purée*
*100ml (4fl oz) red wine*
*salt*
*1 cinnamon stick*
*225g (8oz)* kritharaki *pasta or any other pasta shapes*
*75g (3oz)* kefalotiri *or other hard cheese, grated*

Cut the chicken into eight serving pieces and pat it dry with kitchen paper. Season it well with pepper and sprinkle on the oregano.

Heat the oil and butter in a large frying-pan and, when it is hot, fry the chicken pieces over medium heat for about 6 minutes, turning them over and over so that they brown evenly. Remove the chicken from the pan and set the pieces aside.

Fry the onions until they are transparent, then add the garlic and fry for 1–2 minutes more. Stir in the tomatoes and tomato purée and pour on the wine. Season with salt and pepper and add the cinnamon stick. Return the chicken to the pan, bring the sauce to the boil and spoon it over the chicken pieces. Cover the pan and simmer over low heat for 45–55 minutes, turning the chicken pieces in the sauce once or twice. Test the chicken with a skewer to check that it is cooked. The juices that spurt out should be clear, not pink. Taste the sauce and adjust the seasoning if necessary. Remove the cinnamon stick.

Meanwhile, cook the pasta in a large pan of boiling, salted water for 10–12 minutes or until it is just tender. Drain it into a colander and refresh it by running hot water through it. Drain it again and toss it in a heated bowl with the grated cheese.

Arrange the pasta around the outside of a heated serving dish and pile the chicken and its spicy, colourful sauce in the centre. A green salad is a good accompaniment.

---

# CUSTARD PIES

*Bougatses*

For me, *bougatses* and Skyros are inextricably linked, an association that is locked for ever in the memory. We used to buy them every morning, waiting while the baker sifted a cloud of icing sugar and ground cinnamon over the crisp and crackly-brown pastry tops, and over anyone who happened to be within firing range. Then we went off to a *kafenion* to eat our pies, have a coffee and watch the world go by.

### MAKES ABOUT 10 PIES

*400g (14oz) packet filo pastry*
*about 75g (3oz) butter, melted*
*sifted icing sugar, for dusting*
*ground cinnamon, for dusting*

### FILLING
*900ml (1 1/2 pints) milk, or half-and-half milk and single cream*
*strip of thinly pared lemon rind*
*115g (4 1/2 oz) fine semolina*
*3 eggs, beaten*
*175g (6oz) vanilla sugar (see method)*
*1 1/2 tsp vanilla flavouring*

Begin by making the filling. You can do this a day in advance if you wish. Put the milk or milk and cream into a saucepan with the lemon rind and bring it to the boil. Sprinkle on the semolina and quickly stir it in. Stir over low heat until the mixture thickens. Beat the eggs and sugar together. (If you have a jar of sugar in which a vanilla pod has been steeped, so much the better.) Stir the egg mixture into the pan and stir it over low heat until it thickens again. The wooden spoon should leave a trail as you draw it through the mixture. Stir in the vanilla flavouring and remove and discard the lemon rind. Set aside to cool. Place a circle of wetted greaseproof paper on the surface to prevent a crust forming.

When assembling the pies, it is important to work quickly and to keep pastry-in-waiting under wraps (see page 33). Use a large saucer or a tea plate as a template and cut through the layers of pastry sheets. You can use the hour-glass-shaped 'off-cuts' to make a small spinach or cheese pie for the family. My folk call such examples of frugality 'crazy-paving pies'.

Keep out six circles to make the first pie and cover the remainder with a damp cloth. Brush each circle with melted butter, paying particular attention to the edges, and stack them one on top of the other. Put the pan over low heat to keep the fat liquid.

Put 2 heaped tbsp of the filling in the centre of each stack of pastry circles and fold the pastry over to make a half-moon shape. Press the edges firmly together and then brush the pastry on both sides with butter.

Make more pies in the same way until you have used up all the pastry circles and filling.

Place the pies on a greased or a wetted baking sheet and bake them in the oven at 180°C (350°F/Gas 4) for 25 minutes until they are crisp and golden brown. You can, if you wish, turn them half-way through the cooking time.

Dust the tops of the pies generously with sifted icing sugar and then with as much ground cinnamon as you have a taste for. Serve them warm. They reheat perfectly.

# Figs

Much as I feel drawn to the Greek islands in springtime, principally for the wild flowers, I often long to return later in the same year, as dusk falls on the long, hot summer, to enjoy the figs.

Sometimes, if I am staying on a farm, I help to gather them, bright, stripy green or deep, deep purple and still warm from the sun; sometimes a peasant woman will hold out her apron, heavy with fruit, to offer some as a passing gift; and once, in Sparta in the Peloponnese, I even managed to barter chain-store fruit pies (part of a packed lunch from a cruise boat) for a whole bag of heavenly figs. Amazingly, both parties to the transaction were delighted.

Sometimes, anywhere in the islands, in that time-honoured custom that is, perhaps, the Greek equivalent of the Japanese tea ceremony, one will be offered preserved figs, *siko glyko*, sticky sweet and syrupy, to enjoy with a cup of coffee and a glass of water in a sincere gesture of hospitality.

Figs are the highlight of the season on Evia – not fresh, or even bottled, but pale honey-gold and partly dried, packed in see-through boxes that make unbeatable take-home presents. I won't go on; their virtues, and a local Evian recipe, are extolled elsewhere (see page 109).

On Corfu the dried figs take on quite a different character. You might come across them, deep, dark brown, lightly peppered – a surprisingly good combination – and wrapped in vine leaves. Market stalls are piled high with them, neat, round, cake-like shapes tightly covered with paper-crisp dried leaves and tied round and round, parcel-wise with string. I always keep some for Christmas.

But for real fig cake – *sikopitta* – we must turn to Lawrence Durrell's *Prospero's Cell*, in which he tempts us with a mention of Zarian's favourite fig cake, which 'will come later when the autumn figs are literally bursting open with their own ripeness'. Which seems to me reason enough to make the trip!

# SPINACH PIE

## *Spanakopitta*

I can understand people being markedly indifferent to Greek cheese and vegetable pies if their first or only encounter is with a miserly example that's all pastry and not much filling – a travesty of the real thing, in other words.

For irresistible authenticity, try this one, which is traditionally made on Alonissos with mixed wild greens in place of the more familiar spinach.

### SERVES 6

*400g (14oz) packet filo pastry*
*about 75g (3oz) butter, melted*

#### FILLING
*4 tbsp olive oil*
*8 spring onions, trimmed and thinly sliced*
*1kg (2¼lb) spinach, stalks removed, shredded,*
*or use wild greens*
*4 tbsp chopped parsley (flat-leaved variety, if*
*available)*
*225g (8oz) feta cheese, crumbled*
*4 eggs, beaten*
*4 tbsp double cream*
*black pepper*

Begin by making the filling. Heat the oil in a large pan and fry the spring onions over medium heat for 3–4 minutes. Stir in the greens to coat them with oil, cover the pan and simmer gently for 5 minutes, stirring now and again so that the greens collapse and cook evenly.

Lift out the vegetable mixture with a draining spoon, pressing out any excess liquid, transfer it to a mixing bowl and set aside to cool. Stir in the chopped parsley, the cheese, eggs and cream and season with pepper. Mix well to combine all the ingredients thoroughly.

To assemble the pie, brush a baking tin with melted butter. I use my *pastitsio* tin, which is 25 x 18 x 7·5cm (10 x 7 x 3in). When using the filo pastry, the pointers outlined on page 33 apply. Line the tin with the first sheet of pastry, pressing it neatly into the corners. Give it a quick brush with melted

butter, cover it deftly with another pastry sheet and so on until you have an eight-sheet lining. Put the pan over low heat to keep the fat liquid.

Spoon the cooled filling into the pastry case and spread it evenly. Place a filo sheet over the filling, brush it with butter and quickly follow up with seven more buttered pastry sheets. Trim the pastry edges neatly around the top of the tin and brush the top layer with butter. Mark it in serving-sized squares or diamonds, cutting through only the top two sheets, with the point of a knife and sprinkle the top lightly with water to prevent the pastry from curling.

Bake the pie in the oven at 180°C (350°F/Gas 4) for 45–50 minutes, until it is crisp, puffy and deliciously golden. Serve hot, although there are devotees who are just as happy to eat it cold.

---

# EASTER BREAD

## *Tsoureki*

We rented the most adorable old house on Skyros, a wedge-shaped, one-roomed architectural masterpiece crowded against a brilliant blue and white chapel, and almost impossible to find, tucked away in the maze of tiny back streets.

Every evening we happily joined in the local custom of sitting out on the pavement chatting to our neighbours and, as it was Eastertime, occasionally clinking *kokkina avga* (red-dyed eggs) and sharing the traditional Easter breads, *tsourekia*.

### MAKES ONE 750g (1½lb) LOAF

*75g (3oz) butter, softened*
*100g (4oz) sugar*
*2 eggs*
*1 tbsp (1 sachet) instant dried yeast*
*grated rind 1 orange*
*450g (1lb) strong plain flour*
*3 tbsp lukewarm water*
*150ml (¼ pint) lukewarm milk*
*oil, for greasing*
*3 red-dyed hard-boiled eggs (see note)*
*1 egg white, beaten*
*2 tbsp split blanched almonds*

*Pages 106–107: A quiet flower-fringed bay on Skopelos.*

Beat the butter and half of the sugar in a large bowl until the mixture is light and creamy. Beat in the eggs one at a time. Stir the yeast, orange rind and remaining sugar into the flour and mix the water and milk together. Gradually add the flour and the liquid alternately to the creamed mixture, beating all the time. Mix to form a smooth dough and knead it lightly until it is soft and pliable.

Place the dough in an oiled bowl, cover it with a cloth and leave it to rise in a warm place for 1 hour, when it should have doubled in size.

Turn the dough out on to a lightly floured board and knead it lightly, the process known as knocking back.

Divide the dough into three equal pieces and roll them into long ropes, about the thickness of a sausage. Taper the dough gradually at each end. Press together one end of each strip of dough and plait the strips, placing the three eggs at intervals and plaiting around them. Press the other dough ends together. Place the plaited dough on a greased baking sheet, and leave it in a warm place for 1–1½ hours to rise again.

Brush the top of the dough with the beaten egg white and sprinkle with the almonds.

Bake the loaf in the oven at 200°C (400°F/Gas 6) for 30–35 minutes until the bread is golden brown and sounds hollow when the base of the loaf is tapped. Transfer the loaf to a wire rack to cool.

You can make several small, individual-sized loaves from the dough batch – plait them, shape them into a letter S with an egg in each of the hollows or roll one long strip around and around an egg in the centre.

The bread is specially good served with soft *mizithra* goats' cheese and honey.

\* \* \*

In Greece packets of red Easter-egg dye are sold in every pavement kiosk and general store for weeks before the festival. But you can easily improvise by hard-boiling the eggs in water coloured with a few drops of dark red edible food colouring. On no account use commercial dyes, which are not edible.

# FIG AND WALNUT DESSERT

*Sika kai karithia se siropi*

Go to Evia in the autumn and every village store and pavement kiosk will be piled high with boxes of honey-gold dried figs, a match for any you have ever tasted and the perfect take-home present. Plump, round and still unbelievably succulent, they are good just the way they are, but at homes around the islands the figs are simmered with spices and honey and served as a sweet, with coffee and iced water.

## SERVES 10

*450g (1lb) dried or semi-dried figs (see method)*
*175g (6oz) shelled walnuts*
*5 tbsp honey*
*1 tsp ground cinnamon*

The quality of the figs you use is the make-or-break factor in this dish; the tough, sugar-coated and compressed type that is so widely available just won't do. If you can't come home with Evian figs, look in health-food shops for semi-dried ones that are plump, sticky and what my grandmother used to call 'toothsome'.

Split the figs without cutting right through them and fill them with the walnuts. Press the figs together again to enclose the nuts. Arrange them in a single layer in a baking dish that just fits them. My first encounter with this dish was in the village of Ohthonia on Evia, where I saw several kilos of them arranged in rings in a huge aluminium pan, on their way home after an early-morning simmering at the baker's.

Put the honey and cinnamon in a small pan and dissolve it over low heat. Pour on 250ml (8fl oz) water – or you could use white wine – stir well and bring to the boil. Pour the syrup over the figs and bake the dish, uncovered, in the oven at 180°C (350°F/Gas 4) for 30–35 minutes or until all the liquid has been absorbed. Leave the figs to cool in the tin.

You can store the figs in an airtight box in the refrigerator, although they are best served at warm room temperature. Packed in wax paper cases in a box, they make a scrumptious home-cooked gift.

# CHAPTER 7

# Corfu and Ionia

Corfu, by far the most popular of the Greek islands, is one of sharp contrasts and well-kept secrets. Caught up in any one of the busy resorts, you could be forgiven for thinking that the real Corfu, the one Lawrence Durrell loved so well, had sunk in a tidal wave of tourism. And yet only a few minutes away, by bicycle, by car or even on foot, you come across endearingly remote villages that have a completely unselfconscious and unexploited charm.

For me, Corfu will always be associated with festivities, perhaps because we have spent many a memorable Easter with our friends there, sharing the family's Lenten fare, attending the Good Friday service at the monastery together and eating spit-roast goat in an olive grove by the sea. I write about this most moving of religious festivals in more detail on pages 127–8.

And then there are the village weddings. You could be enjoying a coffee and a cheese pie in the *kafenion* in Liapades when the whole romantic scene unfolds before you. Three musicians, playing a lilting tune, jig their way up the hill and into the square, leading the bridegroom and his entourage to church. Back they go for the bride and her family and friends, while the bridesmaids carry a pleated net canopy swathed in flowers and offer bags of sugared almonds to onlookers.

And again in Valanion, a hillside village that time and tourism have completely ignored, quite by chance you could come across a wedding party in the square, the trestle tables set with salads, plates of *moustalevria*, a spicy grape juice and semolina dessert, and jugs of wine, with several lambs roasting on spits and a bandstand raised up in the centre.

After the meal a troupe of high-kicking men in black breeches and waistcoats gets the dancing off to an exuberant start, until the groom leads his bride and the whole party – bystanders included – in the traditional wedding dance. It's an experience to remember.

*Opposite: Nets are spread to catch every precious olive on Corfu. Below: A* yia-yia, *a delightful Corfiot grandmother, proudly shows off her Filo Custard Pie,* galactoboureko; *recipe on page 120.*

Paxos, a short but often choppy ferry-ride from Corfu, regularly goes *en fête* on Dormiton Day, 15 August (the Feast of the Assumption), when, after the pilgrimage, the celebrations go on well into the night. It's an island of wild flowers – masses of them – and game, olives and vines.

Further south, Lefkas, which is linked to the mainland by a bridge, clings to its homely traditions. The coast road is alight with lemon trees, fishermen's houses built on stilts give shade to cafés underneath and there is the glisten of salt all around – for its collection represents one of the island's main industries. Every strip of land seems to be cultivated with vines, olives, almonds, oranges, broad beans, whatever. A man walks by with a turkey under each arm, and people, sitting on brass-studded donkey saddles, chat in their doorways.

I haven't counted them, but there are said to be 365 villages on Cephallonia, in any of which, I wager, the visitor will be offered one of the local specialities – nougat, honey, praline, quince paste, honey cakes, soft goats' cheese and white Robola wine.

Ithaca, which achieved fame if not fortune as the island of Odysseus' dreams, is a haven of still-unspoilt villages surrounded by vineyards and olive groves, and Zakinthos, or Zante, which lies off the coast of the Peloponnese, is evocatively known as 'the flower of the Levant'. Famous for centuries for its raisins and currants, the island has other specialities, too – sesame seed biscuits and *mandalato*, a type of nougat – and if you keep very still at dusk you just might be privileged to see the giant sea turtles lumbering in from the sea to lay their eggs in the warm sand.

---

# CHICK-PEA PURÉE

## *Hummus*

The west coast of Lefkas, the seaward side of the island, is almost unbelievably beautiful, with its cascades of olive and pear groves, terraced vines, tumbling banks of thyme, meadows of wild flowers and clusters of blue-and-green-striped beehives.

And somewhere there, on a rickety table in her garden, an old lady, swathed in the dark brown skirt and shawl costume of the islanders, was pounding cooked chick-peas with a stone pestle and mortar for this traditional *meze* or first course.

### SERVES 6

*225g (8oz) chick-peas, soaked overnight and drained*
*3 cloves garlic, crushed*
*4 tbsp olive oil, plus more to serve*
*juice of 2 lemons*
*225g (8oz) tahini (sesame seed paste)*
*salt and black pepper*
*$\frac{1}{4}$–$\frac{1}{2}$ tsp ground cumin*
*1 tbsp chopped parsley (flat-leaved variety, if available)*
*lemon wedges, to serve*
*pitta bread*

Cook the chick-peas in a large pan of unsalted water for 1–1¼ hours, until they are tender. The precise time will depend on the age and state of dehydration of the peas. Drain them into a colander and, reserving a few to garnish, put them into a blender or food processor with the garlic, olive oil, lemon juice and *tahini*. Add 150ml (¼ pint) water and blend to a smooth paste. (It may be necessary to process the peas in two batches.) Add a little more water if needed, to make a firm but scoopable purée. Season the mixture with salt, pepper and cumin to your taste.

Turn the pâté into a serving dish and drizzle a little olive oil over the top – just enough to make it glisten. Sprinkle on the chopped parsley and garnish with the reserved chick-peas. Serve with lemon wedges and warm pitta bread.

---

# GRILLED FISH WITH GARLIC SAUCE

## *Psari me skorthalia kai amigthala*

After an all-day drive to Lefkas we booked a table – well, there were only two – at a minuscule taverna in Vassiliki while we went off to find a room.

When we returned, our meal was ready – a welcoming ouzo, grilled *sviritha* fish steaks, a local delicacy, a pungent and creamy garlic and almond sauce, lightly simmered wild greens, crumbly slices of feta cheese, mounds of shiny black olives and a bottle of potent Santa Mavra wine. And all for the price of a plate of cod and chips at home.

### SERVES 4

*4 white fish steaks, such as halibut or turbot,
175–200g (6–7oz) each
salt and black pepper
oil, for brushing
juice of 1 lemon
1 tbsp dried thyme
about 12 bay leaves
4 tbsp chopped parsley (flat-leaved variety, if
available)
2 medium onions, thinly sliced into rings
lemon wedges, to serve*

### SAUCE
*1 large potato, about 175g (6oz)
salt
175g (6oz) coarsely ground almonds or use
walnuts
8 cloves garlic, crushed
juice of 1 lemon
200ml (6fl oz) olive oil*

First make the sauce – another version of *skorthalia*. Cook the potato in boiling, salted water until it is tender – or cook an extra one when you are serving potatoes at another time. Mash the potato thoroughly and beat in the ground almonds or walnuts and crushed garlic – I find a fork does this most satisfactorily. Gradually add the lemon juice and oil, at first adding only a few drops at a time and then increasing the pace. Beat thoroughly all the time, as if you were making mayonnaise. Cover the sauce and set it aside for at least 1 hour for the flavours to blend.

Pre-heat the grill to high. Season the fish on both sides with salt and pepper and brush one side liberally with oil. Sprinkle half the lemon juice and half the dried thyme on to one side of the fish. Cover the grill rack with bay leaves and place the fish on top, seasoned side up.

Reduce the heat to medium and grill the fish for 4–5 minutes. Turn the fish, brush the other side with oil and sprinkle with lemon juice and thyme. Continue grilling the fish until it is just firm – it should flake easily when prodded with a fork.

Line a heated serving dish or individual plates with the chopped parsley and onion rings and place the fish on top. Garnish with the lemon wedges and serve the sauce separately.

Lots of fresh, country-style bread is a must.

## Sage

Sage, which is classified as an evergreen sub-shrub, has a long Hellenic pedigree, having been listed as a medicinal and culinary herb by Theophrastus in his writings on plants. The Romans appreciated its many properties, too; its generic name derives from the Latin *salveo*, to be well.

Throughout the ages, sage leaves and the oil derived from them have been used in the treatment of nervous ailments and of chest, throat and skin troubles, and as an antiseptic. My own experience in this regard – which I touch on in another section – is limited to the dutiful enjoyment of sage tea made for us in Rhodes 'now that winter has come', and a delightful encounter with sage leaves and flowering stems used as a fragrant and air-freshening strewing herb on the floor of a chapel on Amorgos.

The tastiest culinary encounter I have had with the herb was also in the Cyclades, where the proprietor of a small taverna served particularly pungent sausages made, it seemed to me, of pork and sage in almost equal proportions.

In lighter vein, the fruit or, to be exact, galls of the variety *S. pomifera*, which means apple-bearing, is sometimes eaten by children to quench their thirst, and collected on *Protomayia*, the first of May, to be candied and eaten as a sweetmeat.

## FISH KEBABS

### *Souvlakia psariou*

Fish kebabs, as Greek as the blue and red fishing boats moored in the harbour, can be all things to all people. You can pack the skewers from end to end with nothing but moist and tangy chunks of fish or vary the flavours and textures – the colour, too – by adding tiny blanched onions, tomatoes, pepper slices, button mushrooms and even succulent courgettes.

### SERVES 6

*1kg (2¼lb) thick end of white fish fillet, such as*
*cod or haddock, skinned*
*2 courgettes, sliced into 2·5cm (1in) pieces*
*100g (4oz) small button mushrooms, trimmed*
*1 green pepper, cored, seeded and cut into*
*4cm (1½in) squares*
*6 small bay leaves*
*lemon wedges, to serve*

### MARINADE
*8 tbsp olive oil*
*2 tbsp clear honey*
*juice of 2 lemons*
*2 bay leaves, crumbled*
*salt and black pepper*
*1 tbsp chopped parsley*

Mix all the marinade ingredients in a shallow dish.

Wash and dry the fish and cut it into 2·5–4cm (1–1½in) cubes. Put the fish into the marinade, stir to coat it thoroughly and cover the dish. Set aside for at least 2 hours, stirring once or twice if possible.

Thread the fish, courgettes, mushrooms, pepper and bay leaves on to six oiled skewers, alternating the various colours and textures. Brush the kebabs with some of the remaining marinade.

Brush the grill rack with oil and pre-heat the grill to high. Arrange the kebabs on the rack, reduce the heat to medium and grill the kebabs for 5 minutes. Baste them with the remaining marinade, turn them and grill for a further 4–5 minutes until the fish is just firm. It should flake easily when prodded with a fork.

*Right: Fish Kebabs.*

# LEG OF LAMB WITH PASTA

## *Yiouvetsi*

The most come-hither of cooking smells were wafting out of a weather-beaten cottage on Cephallonia as we sat chatting on the terrace with three kindly and elderly sisters.

After a while they invited us into the living-room to see 'our lovely new purchase' – an electric cooker. There it stood, in all its glory, protected by a hand-made lace cloth and garnished with a colourful bunch of meadow flowers. The real work was being done, as it had been for generations, on a wood fire in the corner, where an aluminium pan was hissing and spitting with that most traditional of springtime dishes, *yiouvetsi*.

### SERVES 6

*1 leg of lamb, about 2kg (4½ lb)*
*2 cloves garlic, thinly sliced lengthways*
*salt and black pepper*
*2 tsp dried oregano*
*4 tbsp olive oil*
*450g (1lb) canned tomatoes, chopped*
*225g (8oz) kritharaki or other pasta shapes*
*300ml (½ pint) boiling water*
*2 tbsp chopped oregano or mint*
*50g (2oz) kefalotiri or other hard cheese, grated*

Make slits in the lamb and press in slivers of garlic. Season the meat on all sides with salt, pepper and the oregano, pour the oil into a roasting pan and place the meat in the centre. Tip in the tomatoes and cook the meat in the oven at 220°C (425°F/Gas 7) for 45 minutes. During this time turn the meat once and spoon the tomatoes over it.

Meanwhile, blanch the pasta in boiling, salted water for 3 minutes. Drain it into a colander and refresh it by running hot water through it. Pour the 300ml (½ pint) boiling water around the meat, then spoon the pasta evenly into the water and stir well.

Reduce the oven heat to 190°C (375°F/Gas 5) and continue cooking for a further 45–60 minutes, according to how rare or well done you like the meat to be.

Stir the pasta occasionally during this time to prevent it from sticking and turn the meat once more.

Transfer the lamb to a heated serving dish. Taste the pasta and tomato mixture, adjust the seasoning if necessary and stir in the chopped herb. Spoon the pasta around the meat and sprinkle it with the grated cheese. Serve, ideally, with a well-chilled green salad.

---

# BRAISED BEEF

## *Stifatho*

We had ventured, with only-just-adequate scooter power, way into the Corfiot mountains, helped an old lady in a remote village to gather in a goodly supply of firewood, gazed in awe at the massive snow-capped peaks of neighbouring Albania, and bought a packet of lentils to make soup – for, shiveringly, it was that kind of weather.

Picture our gratitude, then, when our friend Chrissa greeted us with a huge, fiery red pot of *stifatho*, as warm and welcoming as could be.

### SERVES 4–6

*6 tbsp olive oil*
*1kg (2 ¼lb) stewing steak, cubed*
*2 medium onions, sliced*
*3 cloves garlic, finely chopped*
*4 tbsp tomato purée*
*200ml (6fl oz) red wine*
*3 tbsp red wine vinegar*
*2 tsp sugar*
*½ tsp cloves*
*½ tsp cumin seeds*
*2 bay leaves*
*1 cinnamon stick*
*salt and black pepper*
*450g (1lb) small onions or shallots*
*1 tbsp lemon juice*
*2 tbsp chopped coriander or parsley*

Heat half the oil in a flameproof casserole (or you could use a large pan and transfer the ingredients to an oven dish) and fry the meat over medium heat, stirring from time to time, until it is evenly browned. It might be necessary to do this in two batches. Lift out the meat with a draining spoon and set it aside.

Heat the remaining oil and fry the onions over medium heat until they are transparent. Add the garlic and fry for 1–2 minutes more. Stir in the tomato purée, wine, vinegar and sugar and return the meat to the dish or pan. Tie the cloves and cumin seeds into a small piece of muslin and add them to the dish with the bay leaves and cinnamon. Season the sauce with salt and pepper and cover the dish.

Cook in the oven at 170°C (325°F/Gas 3) for 1½ hours, stirring once or twice.

Blanch the small onions in boiling, salted water for 1 minute, then drain them. Stir them into the casserole. Continue cooking for 1–1¼ hours until the meat is tender. Remove the bag of spices, the bay leaves and cinnamon. Stir in the lemon juice, taste the sauce and adjust the seasoning if necessary. Sprinkle on the chopped herb before serving.

# CHICKEN WITH WALNUT SAUCE

*Kotopoulo me saltsa karithiou*

Strangely, my most vivid mind-images of Zakinthos – or Zante, to give the island its Venetian name – both have to do with dancing patterns of light. On the one hand, there is the shimmering, iridescent kaleidoscope of blue on green on silver, as the afternoon sunlight bounces off the sea and on to the craggy walls of the Blue Grotto, making them look for all the world like Impressionist stained glass windows. And then there is the other, so much more homely image of golden lamplight flickering in an isolated farm cottage, where we shared this simple country dish.

## SERVES 4

*2 tbsp flour*
*salt and black pepper*
*2 tsp dried oregano*
*4 chicken pieces, washed and dried*
*3 tbsp olive oil*
*25g (1oz) butter*
*150ml (¼ pint) white wine*
*150ml (¼ pint) chicken stock*
*75g (3oz) shelled walnuts (see method)*
*1 tbsp chopped coriander or parsley*

Season the flour with salt, pepper and the oregano. Toss the chicken in the flour to coat it thoroughly, then shake off any excess.

Heat the oil and butter in a large pan and fry the chicken pieces over medium heat until they are golden brown on both sides – which will take about 10 minutes in all.

Pour in the wine and stock and season with salt and pepper. Spoon the liquid over the chicken, cover the pan and simmer for 55–60 minutes or until the chicken is cooked. Turn the chicken pieces in the sauce once during that time. Test that the chicken is cooked by piercing the thick part of a leg with a skewer. Any juices that spurt out should be clear, not pink.

If you can obtain fresh or 'wet' walnuts in autumn, the taste of the sauce will be incomparably better, but dried ones are just as traditional. Either grind the walnuts to a 'coarse minced' texture in a blender or food processor, or roughly chop them and pound them with a pestle and mortar.

Transfer the chicken pieces to a heated serving dish, cover and keep them warm. Stir the walnuts into the sauce and simmer for 5 minutes until the sauce has thickened. Taste and adjust the seasoning if necessary. Pour the sauce over the chicken and sprinkle it with the chopped herb.

Serve with potatoes boiled in their skins and a plain vegetable. Cauliflower is especially good.

*Left: Fig cake, dried figs wrapped in leaves, and the irresistible fresh fruit displayed on a Corfiot hillside. Above: Posies of wild garden flowers are bound into a circlet for the* Protomayia stefani. *Top: Sparkling with freshness, strawberries are sometimes served with ouzo on Corfu at Eastertime; recipe on page 120.*

## FILO CUSTARD PIE

### *Galactoboureko*

I had my first lesson in making *galactoboureko* on Corfu, when 18-year-old Magda and her delightful grandmother, the *yia-yia*, first showed me how to roll out tissue-paper-thin filo pastry. The instruction took place on a table moved to a shady part of the garden, for on that day in Paleokastritsa it was too hot to work in the kitchen.

My second attempt was at Christmastime, when Magda and her younger sister Georgia stayed with us and proved to be the most effervescent and giggly tutors I have ever had the pleasure to work with!

### SERVES 12

*400g (14oz) packet filo pastry*
*about 75g (3oz) butter, melted*

### CUSTARD
*1 litre (1³/₄ pints) milk*
*large pinch of salt*
*225g (8oz) vanilla sugar (see method)*
*140g (5¹/₂ oz) fine semolina*
*6 eggs, beaten*
*2 tsp vanilla flavouring*

### SYRUP
*225g (8oz) sugar*
*juice of 1 lemon*
*strip of thinly pared lemon rind*
*1 cinnamon stick*

First, make the custard. Pour the milk into a pan. Add the salt and sugar – best of all, sugar that has had a vanilla pod steeped in it – and bring slowly to the boil. Stir from time to time until the sugar has dissolved. Tip in the semolina and stir it in quickly, using a wooden spoon. Stir the mixture over a low heat for 5 minutes.

Remove the pan from the heat and beat in the eggs and vanilla. Cover the surface with a piece of wetted greaseproof paper to prevent a skin forming on the custard and set aside to cool.

Assemble the pie in a large baking dish. The *yia-yia* used a round aluminium pan 25cm (10in) across. Cover the base of the pan with the first sheet of pastry, bringing it up and over the sides and brush

it with butter. Keep the rest of the pastry covered with a damp cloth (see page 33). Working as quickly as you can to prevent the pastry from drying out, place another five sheets of pastry in the dish, brushing each one with butter. Put the pan over a low heat to keep the fat liquid.

Pour the cooled filling into the dish and level the top. Cover the filling with six sheets of butter-brushed pastry. Trim the edges neatly and score through the top two sheets in a diamond pattern – more for traditional decoration than for serving. Brush the top with butter again and bake the pie in the oven at 180°C (350°/Gas 4) for 45–50 minutes until the pastry is crisp and golden brown and the custard is set. A skewer inserted in the centre should come out clean. Leave the pie to cool.

To make the syrup, put the sugar, lemon juice, lemon rind and cinnamon into a pan with 250ml (8fl oz) water. Bring slowly to the boil, stirring occasionally until the sugar has dissolved. Boil rapidly for 10 minutes, then set aside until it is lukewarm.

Remove the lemon rind and cinnamon and pour the syrup slowly and carefully over the pie. Leave the pie until all the syrup has been absorbed. Serve it with ice-cold water to counteract the sticky sweetness of it all.

---

## STRAWBERRIES IN OUZO

### *Fraoules me ouzo*

It seems to be the done thing to bring home a souvenir bottle of ouzo from a trip to Greece. And yet somehow – put it down to a less favourable ambience, a different climate, what you will – the aperitif just doesn't have the same appeal.

So here's the perfect solution. A dessert that makes use of the redundant bottle of spirit, puts a zip into a plate of strawberries and, for me at least, evokes fond memories of a joyous Easter Day meal prepared for us by friends in Paleokastritsa, Corfu.

### SERVES 6

*1kg (2¹/₄lb) strawberries*
*50–75g (2–3oz) icing sugar*
*150ml (¹/₄ pint) ouzo*

Reserve a few of the showiest berries for decoration. Hull and thickly slice the rest and, if you have the patience, arrange them in concentric rings around a serving dish. My dear friend Chrissa made a work of art of her arrangement, with the largest slices and all of the same size in the outer ring, smallest ones in the centre.

Sift the sugar over the berries – the amount you need will depend on the sweetness of the fruit and on your individual taste. Pour on the ouzo, cover with film or foil and chill for at least 2 hours.

Arrange the whole berries in a cluster in the centre – a few small strawberry or herb leaves, too, if you have them – and serve chilled.

Shortbread or walnut biscuits (see page 124) go well with this simple but elegant dish.

## Filo Pastry

You need only four ingredients to make those paper-thin sheets of filo pastry that turn into such divine pies: plain flour, baking powder, water and patience. Oh, and a large flat surface, although it need not be as large as I at first imagined. My earliest attempt at making filo, when I thought the done thing was to roll out the whole batch in one go, was a disaster. I ended up with pastry that was, more or less, as thin as tissue paper, but unfortunately as it was hanging over the sides of the table like a limp grey cloth, it was stretching uncontrollably all the while.

You will need 1kg (2¼lb) plain flour; 10ml (2 tsp) baking powder and cold water – the exact amount will depend on the brand of flour you use.

Sift the flour and baking powder into a bowl and sprinkle on just enough water to make a stiff dough. Knead the dough lightly until it is smooth, then cover it and set it aside for 2 hours.

Break the dough into pieces about the size of a tennis ball. And after that, as far as rolling and stretching it goes, there comes a parting of the ways. Most people I know – my friend Magda and her grandmother included – are content to roll out the dough with a rolling pin on a lightly floured surface until each piece is as thin, and evenly so, as possible. As one jovial pastry cook described it to me, the dough should be so thin that you can read a newspaper through it.

Talking of jovial pastry cooks, I once spent a merry morning in a filo factory in Kerkira town, watching the toss and thrust, twist and twirl actions of the professionals. Their agility and accuracy in swinging and balancing the dough, like some gyrating pancake, has to be seen to be believed – and then, if you have the courage perhaps, attempted.

Cover each piece of rolled-out dough with a damp tea towel, stacking one piece on top of another until you have worked through the batch. Then, if you do not want to use them straight away, roll or concertina-fold the pastry sheets and wrap and seal them in polythene. Store the dough in the refrigerator or in the freezer. As the pastry is so thin, it takes only minutes to thaw.

On the other hand, of course, you could do what most very accomplished cooks do and buy your filo in packets from the grocer or from a supermarket.

*Above: The Corfu that so many visitors to the island never discover. A hillside village shimmers in the noonday sun. Right: Baked Quinces are a speciality at the Lucciola Inn, Sgombou, Corfu.*

# BAKED QUINCES

*Kithonia sto fourno*

It was one of those live-forever-in-the-memory occasions. Twelve or fourteen of us were revelling in a family birthday celebration at a country inn in Corfu. And as we relished our way through a *meze* of dried beans in tomato sauce, aubergine fritters, fried cheese, pickled beetroot, artichokes in cheese sauce, tuna fish in bean salad, roasted red peppers and herb-packed meatballs, there was, distractingly, this alluring smell wafting past our noses.

It turned out to be the speciality of the house, baked quinces, on their way to first one table and then another. We couldn't resist them.

### SERVES 4

*4 large, ripe quinces*
*at least 8 tbsp clear honey*

This is a dish that turns the ripest, yellowest, mellowest of fruits into pure ambrosia. It doesn't work wonders on tough, resistant, under-ripe specimens, so the selection of the fruit is everything.

Wipe the quinces with a damp cloth and prick the skins all over with a fine skewer. Wrap them closely in foil and place them, upright, in a baking dish that just fits them. Cook them in the oven at 220°C (425°F/Gas 7) for 1¼–1½ hours, depending on the size and ripeness of the fruit.

Unwrap the quinces and drizzle them with honey. You can, if you wish, add lemon wedges to serve.

It's a matter of taste whether guests choose to eat the skin of the fruit. Most Greeks, I'm told, find it rather bitter and are adept at performing a neat surgical operation with a knife and fork. But it seems to me that you waste honey that way.

# WALNUT BISCUITS

## *Kourambiedes*

Friends on Paxos, like most Greeks I suppose, can't contemplate the thought of Christmas without a never-ending supply of these traditional shortbread biscuits. And so one year they packed up a couple of kilos – yes, it was a massive box – and posted them to us as a timely surprise gift.

Unfortunately … well, you can guess the rest. But I can report that the crumbled biscuits, icing sugar and all, stirred into half-yoghurt, half-cream and with a dash of brandy made the most heavenly Christmas dinner ice-cream.

### MAKES ABOUT 24 BISCUITS

*225g (8oz) butter, softened*
*75g (3oz) icing sugar, sifted, plus more for dusting*
*1 tsp vanilla flavouring*
*1 egg yolk, beaten*
*450g (1lb) plain flour*
*1 tsp baking powder*
*75g (3oz) walnuts, chopped*

Beat the butter and sugar until it is pale and creamy, then beat in the vanilla and egg yolk. Sift together the flour and baking powder and gradually stir it into the creamed mixture. Stir in the walnuts and gather up the mixture to form a ball of dough. Knead it lightly to remove cracks.

Break off large-walnut-sized pieces of the dough and shape them into rounds. Place them well apart on a non-stick or a greased and floured baking sheet. Bake in the oven at 180°C (350°F/Gas 4) for 20–25 minutes until the biscuits turn light brown at the edges.

Transfer the biscuits to a wire rack to cool, then coat them liberally – and I do mean liberally – in icing sugar. Store in an airtight tin.

## New Year's Eve

St Basil, the patron saint of the Greek new year, is the Orthodox Greek equivalent of St Nicholas or Santa Claus. He has a similarly endearing habit of going from house to house distributing presents from a sleigh, and his generosity is usually acknowledged by a large slice of *vasilopitta*, the special new year's cake.

It goes without saying that new year's eve is an occasion for a big family party, when friends and relatives are greeted with spoon sweets, coffee and *kourambiedes*, those crisp and crumbly, icing-sugar-covered walnut biscuits (see this page), which are made in quantity for the festive season.

These traditional symbols of hospitality are usually followed by a large buffet supper and then, on the stroke of midnight, by the cutting of the cake, a large yeast-risen dome, which can be flavoured with cinnamon or orange.

Church bells ring, fireworks may be let off in the gardens, and guests wish each other *Hronia polla*, many happy years. The host makes the sign of the cross over the cake, sets aside the first slice for the Holy Mother or for St Basil, and then serves guests in order of seniority. It's a time of tense excitement, to see who has the lucky silver or golden coin in his or her slice. If it is found to be in the first slice, good fortune showers on the whole assembly, but if it is in the cake that's left over – by tradition to be distributed to the poor – that's as it should be.

The ceremony of the cake is naturally accompanied by a celebration drink, perhaps champagne or its equivalent, and, with luck, it will be interrupted by a well-wishing first-footer, traditionally a tall, blond and handsome man.

# PRESERVED KUMQUATS

*Kumkuat koutaliou*

I always find it deeply touching, whenever I am offered a 'spoon sweet', the traditional symbol of warm hospitality, in a Greek household. As with most time-honoured customs, it's as well to know the form, so that you can play your part with equal grace. The host or hostess brings in a tray with a jar or bowl of the preserve – it may consist of figs, grapes, cherries, cubes of pumpkin, kumquats or whatever the local crops yield – and a glass of water, a spoon and a cup of coffee for each guest.

You are expected to take a spoonful of the preserve, eat it, then drink the glass of water and place the spoon in the empty glass. Then drink the coffee and, if it is also offered, the glass of *raki* or liqueur. If your Greek isn't up to expressing your thanks – *epharisto poli* – be sure to put on your friendliest smile.

On Corfu, kumquats are the sunniest and most prolific of crops, and they are frequently offered in this way.

### MAKES 1kg (2 ½lb)

*1kg (2¼lb) sugar*
*1kg (2¼lb) kumquats*
*juice of 2 lemons*
*strip of thinly pared lemon rind*
*3–4 drops vanilla flavouring*

Put the sugar into a large pan, pour on 450ml (³⁄4 pint) water and bring slowly to the boil, stirring occasionally until the sugar has dissolved.

Remove any stems from the kumquats and prick the fruit all over with a sterilized darning needle, so that the syrup can penetrate the skins. Add the kumquats, lemon juice, lemon rind and vanilla to the syrup, bring to the boil and boil for 5 minutes.

Transfer the contents of the pan to a large mixing bowl and leave overnight. (Do not leave the fruit for any length of time in a metal pan.)

The next day, return the fruit and syrup to the pan, bring to the boil and simmer until the kumquats are soft. This may take about 1 hour.

Lift out the fruit with a draining spoon and pack it into warm, sterilized jars. Boil the syrup until it is thick. At this stage, half a teaspoon of syrup dropped on to a cold plate should hold its shape and not spread. Discard the lemon rind.

Pour the syrup over the fruit to cover it and close the jars. Store in a cool place.

---

# GRAPE JUICE DESSERT

*Moustalevria*

Everyone on Ithaca, it seems, has a few vines. Pale, translucent yellowy-green in late spring, rich, vibrant emerald green through summer, and golden brown and heavy with dark fruit in autumn. That's when the islanders are busy treading and pressing the grapes, turning many a cottage into a mini-winery.

But not all the grape juice goes into the production of wine. Some of the deep, deep, glowing crimson liquid is siphoned off to make this fragrant dessert. For those of us who are not lucky enough to 'have a few vines', bottled or canned grape juice does just as well.

### SERVES 4

*600ml (1 pint) red grape juice*
*50g (2oz) sugar*
*¼ tsp ground cinnamon, plus more for dusting*
*60g (2½oz) fine semolina*
*4 tbsp Greek yoghurt*
*4 tbsp chopped walnuts*

Put the grape juice, sugar and cinnamon into a small pan and bring slowly to the boil, stirring from time to time. Sprinkle on the semolina and quickly stir it in, using a wooden spoon. Stir the mixture, still over low heat, until it bubbles and thickens. Simmer it very slowly for 4–5 minutes, stirring occasionally.

Pour the dessert into four individual bowls and leave it to cool and set.

Swirl the yoghurt over each dessert, scatter with the nuts and dust with just as much cinnamon as you have a taste for. Serve chilled.

# The Greek Orthodox Easter

To celebrate Easter in Greece is to experience a see-saw of emotions from deep solemnity to pure happiness. First, there is the long build-up to Easter Day which, because the Greek Orthodox calendar is calculated by a different method, does not necessarily coincide with the Anglican festival. There is the 40-day Lenten period with the fervour of the religious services and the processions, the discipline of the dietary abstention, and the frenzy of the preparations. As families travel from far and wide to be at home for the celebrations, the workload in the kitchen is daunting but something that no mother or grandmother would miss for the world.

Almost every Greek family cooks lamb or goat for Easter. In a small household it may be a casserole or a roast, such as *yiovetsi*, roast lamb with pasta, for which there is a recipe on page 116. But whenever there is a large enough gathering, the choice will always be for a whole animal, spit-roast in the garden, in the street outside or – a popular choice on the islands – way out in the countryside.

An awesome number of young lambs and kid goats are bred specially for the occasion and – it has to be faced – slaughtered for it, too. In country regions or wherever they have the facilities, families will buy their Pascal lamb or goat 'on the hoof' and keep it in the garden or in a shed for a few days before the butcher, *hasapis*, makes his rounds. The squeamish must beware of coming across the harshest of realities, the act of ritual slaughter, which takes place at the very entrance to each house. This done, the butcher dips a cloth in the animal's blood, makes the sign of the cross on the wall as a symbol of good fortune and happiness for Easter, and takes the carcass away to hang and dress it.

Holy Saturday, the Day Minus One, reminds me of Christmas Eve at home, but with warmth and sunshine. There's a universal smell of baking, as trays of bread and biscuits are taken from the oven; last-minute supplies of fresh fruit and vegetables are brought in from the market; chocolate rabbits, ducks and chickens are hidden from the children; the *kokkina avga*, red-dyed eggs (see page 118) are polished with olive oil (usually the children's job); and one by one the salads and side dishes are prepared and set aside.

On Corfu there is a special and unique highlight to the day. On Easter Saturday morning people from all over the island make their way to Kerkira town, jostling for a vantage point. Buildings are draped with red – flags, blankets, rugs, anything – balloon sellers do a vigorous trade, and an air of expectancy ripples back and forth through the crowds. More people than one would think possible gather on the balconies of all the shops and dwellings in the town, and on the stroke of 11 o'clock the term 'throwing a pot' is given new meaning. In an act that symbolizes the betrayal of Jesus Christ by Judas, people

*Opposite: The solemn Easter procession passes through Spianada, in the centre of Kerkira town, Corfu.*
*Below: Tsourekia, Easter breads, which may be baked around a red-dyed egg; recipe on page 108.*

drop or throw a hail of earthenware pots on to the street below. Some are filled with water, some with fibre, and while onlookers are kept at a safe distance, the pots crash to the ground, and the spectacle is all over in a flash. The street cleaners move in, the marching bands, like players in a comic opera, weave their way noisily through the maze of streets, and the town goes 'carnival'.

And then, at home again and in the tavernas, it is time to make the *magiritsa*, the traditional offal and vegetable soup that is eaten in the early hours of Easter Day to break the Lenten fast. While it is in preparation the dish does not look too promising, as heaps of well-washed intestines, like slippery spaghetti, the heart, lights and fat of the Pascal animal are chopped, blanched and put into a casserole. The liver and kidneys are never added; they are far too precious. Sliced onions, lettuce hearts and leeks follow, there's a lavish seasoning of salt, pepper and herbs, and the pot is topped up with water and put to simmer for four or five hours, to be ready when the family returns from church.

As midnight approaches, people make their way to churches all over the country, stopping to buy devotional candles – some gaily festooned with ribbons and toys for the children – from roadside stalls. As the clock strikes 12, all the lights in the town or village are extinguished, and a hush that one can hear and feel spreads throughout the open-air congregation.

It is Easter Day! A firework breaks the spell. Neighbours in the crowd embrace and exchange the greeting of the faithful, *Christos anesti!*, Christ has risen! A procession of bishops, priests and other dignitaries leaves the church, carrying light, the symbol of the Resurrection, to the people. Candles are lit one from the other, hand to hand, throughout the throng, and it is like the coming of a new and emotionally charged dawn.

Eventually the crowd disperses, in deep concentration, hands cupped over the flickering candle flames. For the very best of luck it is important to keep the flame

burning all the way home, and to burn a sign of the cross over the front door, which plays havoc with the paintwork.

The Lenten fast is over, the *magiritsa* is ready – and proves to be delicious – and so are the red eggs. Everyone cups one in his hand, clinks it with his neighbour's and so on round the table. At our first Greek Easter our host told us it was a case of winner takes – and eats – all. With 12 eggs in play, and all well and truly hard-boiled, I made sure that mine was comprehensively cracked at the first blow.

No matter how long the festival meal lasts as the wine flows and the dancing gathers pace, there's a bright and early start to the main business of the day. The fire in the barbecue pit is lit, the animal put on to roast, and everyone takes a lucky turn at the spit. There might be a small portable barbecue sizzling with the reserved offal, and with small lamb chops, sweetbreads and salami for the host to offer to visitors.

At last the meal is ready and the spit is carried shoulder-high to a table for the meat to be chopped into only-just-manageable pieces that must, by convention, be eaten in the fingers. There may be a pause for a celebratory toast, and then the meal begins in earnest with, perhaps, bowls of radishes, olives, beans and peppers; slices of feta and other cheeses; and cods' roe salad, chick-pea purée, aubergine salad and hunks of slightly sour-tasting bread. Glasses are filled with the best home-made wine, or even champagne, and gifts are exchanged. Still to come are baskets of fruit, all those home-made cakes and biscuits, and yet more wine. The meal ends. The dancing begins. And, as one dear old Corfiot lady told me confidentially, 'some of us fall happily asleep among the flowers'.

# A Taste of Greek Wines

Selecting a bottle of rich, ruby-red wine to enjoy with a country casserole, or a clear, sparkling honey-gold vintage to complement a plate of fish cooked straight from the sea; clinking glass after glass of young 'green' wine at a vineyard tasting in the Peloponnese, where so much of the country's output is produced; helping to tumble huge wine barrels part-filled with stones (the traditional way of cleaning them) back and forth over cobbles in a Corfiot hamlet; sharing bronze mugs of heady home-made wine (the essential prelude to a round of joyous dancing) at a village wedding on Skyros; chilling bottles of retsina in an ice-cold stream on Andros in anticipation of a country picnic; even buying a bottle or two of Greek wine from a supermarket back home – for many of us so much of the glory that is Greece is captured in her distinctive wines.

Viticulture is one of the country's oldest skills, whose origins are, truly, obscured by the mists of time. It is known that wine has been produced in Greece since Neolithic times, which is to say for some 6,000 years, and that the ancient Greeks worshipped the vine as a form of divinity. Beautiful works of art featuring vineyards, grapes and wine were dedicated to Dionysos, the god of wine and pleasure, and it is worth noting that his standing equalled that of Apollo, the god of the sun, and of Demeter, the goddess of the earth.

The ancient Greeks prided themselves on the quality of their wines and traded them in huge quantities in exchange for Egyptian grain, Spanish silver and Caucasian timber. And it was – perhaps surprisingly – the Greeks who first introduced the grading concept, known as the apellation of origin. Among the most sought-after 'appellations' in antiquity were the gentle wines of Thassos and the more 'rounded' wines of Santorini and Crete.

The geological and climatic characteristics of the country are ideally suited to the production of the vine. The largely alkaline and rocky soils, which are volcanic in places, and the various microclimates experienced from one region – even one vineyard –

to the next guarantee a wide variety of fine wines.

Originally, cultivation was concentrated around the coastal regions, but over the centuries it has spread inland, and vineyards are now a familiar sight on hill- and mountainsides up to a level of 800 metres (2,600 feet). Just over half the country's vineyards, which cover some 186,000 hectares (over 700 square miles), are planted with wine-grape varieties, a timely reminder that Greece is also a major producer of table grapes, currants and sultanas. Of the islands, the main wine-growing areas are on Crete, Rhodes, Santorini, Paros, Samos, Zakinthos, Cephallonia, Lefkas and Corfu, although almost every island community produces its own characteristic local wine that villagers will proudly share with visitors.

In all, about 300 wine-grape varieties are cultivated in Greece, among them the deep blue Mandelaria and the white Vilana grapes, which are grown extensively on Crete; the white Assyrtiko variety, which is cultivated on Santorini and on Mount Athos; the purple Mavrodaphne, which characterizes the red wines of Cephallonia and the Achaia region of the Peloponnese; the fruity white Robola grape, also widely grown on Cephallonia, and the white Savatiano grape, which grows so abundantly on Evia.

That is not to say, however, that the bulk, or even the pride of Greek wines are produced from a single grape variety. Much of the vintners' skill comes in the blending, and wines produced from more than one, strictly defined, variety grown within a well-delineated area qualify for 'apellation' status, under which wines are labelled and marketed with the name of their region of origin.

All these vines, all these grape varieties add up to a total wine production nationwide of 5 million hectolitres (110 million gallons), which is made up of 60 per cent white wines and 40 per cent red and rosé types.

Continuing the proud history of their controlled appellation status, Greek wines now conform with

European Community legislation, and they are categorized as 'table wines' or 'appellation of origin'.

A small quantity of these 'apellation' wines are further upgraded to qualify for the coveted status of 'reserve' (*epilegmenos*) or 'grand reserve' (*eithika epilegmenos*). This means that these matured wines, referred to in Greece as *Cava*, must have been aged in the casks, in conditions of controlled humidity and temperature, for a minimum of two years for whites and three years for reds, which qualifies them for the 'reserve' status, and one year longer in each case to achieve the 'grand reserve' distinction.

## RETSINA

There are fine Greek wines, some may say; there are good Greek wines; and then there is retsina! With its tangy, pine-like aroma and flavour, retsina is certainly an acquired taste, and people fall into two distinct groups: they either love it or they hate it. Retsina is not only characteristic of Greece – the traditional product of both the vineyards and the pine groves – it is unique to that country, since no other EC nation is allowed to produce it.

The wine is either white – by far the more popular choice – or rosé; and don't believe a thing

*Right: Large-scale harvesting of the grape and the olive in a Cretan vineyard. Below: Local island wines are often produced using far more basic methods.*

its detractors may tell you: it is produced with precisely the same technology as other Greek table wines. The only difference is that in the production of retsina small pieces of pine bark are added to the must to give the wine its resinated flavour. Once the bark has fulfilled its purpose and flavoured the wine to a greater or lesser extent, it is removed in filtration.

Why? Whoever first thought of adding pine bark to wine? And why would they do so? I'm glad you asked that. It all dates back to the time when the Greeks stored their wines in goatskins and poured pitch-pine resin over them to seal the seams and make them watertight. This practical measure had far-reaching consequences, in that the pitch seeped into the wine and impregnated it with a most

ungrapelike flavour. When wine casks and bottles were invented, goatskin containers were thrown to the back of the cartsheds, and that could have been an end to it all. But happily it was not. Producers and their customers had come to like the characteristic flavour of their wine, and a way was found of reproducing it, by adding pine bark, with its high concentration of resin, to the process.

For people who, like those early connoisseurs, do enjoy it, retsina is *the* wine to call for at a harbourside taverna in the middle of the morning with a plate of *mezethakia* – what I like to call 'Greek elevenses'. It is the ideal accompaniment to a simple bread, cheese and salad lunch, to take (not forgetting the flip-top bottle opener) on a picnic in the country or on the beach, to carry in a haversack

(for medicinal purposes only, of course) as a restorative on a long country walk or a bicycle ride, to put top of the 'stores' list when preparing to sail around the islands – oh, I could go on and on!

The best of the retsina wines – Retsina Boutari is one – are labelled as other wines are, with the name of the grower and region, and each one has its following. The brand loyalty was brought sternly home to me once when we were giving a Greek-style party. I asked a guest (who knows Greece well) if he would like a glass of retsina, only to be asked, in return, what brand it was. 'I may or may not like a glass of retsina,' he said. 'It depends where it comes from.' Collapse of stout hostess!

Unbranded and unbottled wines, the ones drawn from the wood in local tavernas, have their critics, too, and people will choose to patronize a taverna or not simply on the quality of the house retsina. The barrels are traditionally tapped and the new season's retsina tasted on 26 October, St Demetrius' Day, a day of both serious assessment and noisy carousing in many a wine-growing area.

In local tavernas such as this, the wine is served in bronze-coloured mugs, which is by far the cheapest and most 'local' way to buy it. In certain circumstances, a half-kilo measure, a *misioka*, seems to disappear with remarkable speed.

On other occasions, when you are enjoying a drink in a taverna or *kafenion*, wine and other drinks have a habit of appearing with equal rapidity and quite unexpectedly, too. It can be disconcerting when the waiter brings a bottle of retsina or a glass of ouzo or *raki* that you haven't ordered and, in answer to your query, waves his arm vaguely in one direction or another. It is just another Greek custom. People at neighbouring tables will buy a drink for visitors and expect no thanks or even acknowledgement. If you do discover the identity of your benefactor, don't make the mistake of returning the compliment. It is part of the same old Greek custom that the Greek, on his home territory, will always have the last word!

## THE PELOPONNESE

Patra, on the northwest coast of the Peloponnese, is the home of the longest-established wine-making company in Greece, Achaia Clauss. Visitors may tour the famous factory with its enormous vats and up-to-date wine-making equipment and will be invited to taste some of the large range of wines produced there. These include Patras, Nemea, Château Clauss, Cava Clauss, Danielis, Santa Helena, Bon Viveur and Retsina Liokri. The company also produces an ouzo under its Achaia Clauss brand name.

Once, on a tour of this region, my travels took me way off the beaten track, southeast of Patra, to the village of Demesthika, at the heart of the producer's wine-growing area. It was a good move. Every visitor is treated like an old friend, and it would be considered impolite to leave the labourers to their tasks without accepting their offer to taste one or two of the wines.

Whether Homer enjoyed a similar experience one does not know, but he noted that Methoni, in the Messinian region, was 'rich in vines'. Tradition persists that the town was so named because

donkeys carrying cargoes of wine became intoxicated from the heady aroma.

Moving eastwards, close to Corinth, we happened upon one of those highlights of a day's travelling, a pot of octopus in red wine (I give the recipe on page 12). This was served with the taverna proprietor's home-made red wine, which proved so agreeable that a diner at the next table produced a 50-litre (11-gallon) plastic container from his car and had it filled on the spot, as one does with a *vrac* in France. Encouraged by this unmistakable sign of approval, the amateur producer launched into a lengthy mime, which took us through the harvesting, transporting and treading of the grapes – he rolled up his trousers for the purpose – through testing the sugar content and on, finally, to filling his barrels. And all for the price of a plate of stew!

## THE CYCLADES

The Cyclades were the natural home of the vine in ancient times, and wines were produced on many of the islands, as, indeed, they are today. There are, however, two major wine-growing regions, Santorini and Paros, which, although they are relatively close neighbours, have different soil and climatic conditions and, therefore, produce wines with widely different characteristics.

On Santorini, where the speed of the *meltemi* wind is particularly high, the vines are pruned very low, to form a protective basket shape. The unique quality of the soil, which successive volcanic eruptions have covered with cinders, ash, lava and pumice stone, gives all the island's wines a distinctive 'nose'.

Santorini, or Thera as it is also known, is famous for the cultivation of the rare and indigenous Assyrtiko grape, described by one wine commentator as 'the most extraordinary white grape in all the Mediterranean basin'. One of the finest wines produced from this grape is Santorini Boutari, a high quality dry white wine with an attractive luminosity and a strong character.

An unusual wine known as straw wine and as *liastros* is produced from a blend of the Assyrtiko grape and a Muscat-flavoured variety called Aidani. After harvesting, the grapes are first dried slowly in the sun before being pressed. This means that the must is so rich in natural sugar and ferments so slowly, that no sugar or alcohol is added and the wine is, rightly, called naturally sweet.

On Paros, the two best-known grape varieties are the white Monemvassia, also known as Malvoisie or Malvasia, which makes an outstanding dry white wine, and the red Mandelaria, which makes an excellent red *mistelle*, which is used as a basis in the production of vermouth. The 100-year-old firm of Boutari uses this grape variety to produce Paros Boutari, a mellow, ruby-coloured, dry wine with the true flavour of the Aegean.

## THE DODECANESE

Of all the islands in the Dodecanese group Rhodes has most consistently maintained its historic wine-making tradition. In ancient times the island's wine production was exported in clay amphorae on which the potter stamped the name of the wine and the vintners' trademark, a bunch of grapes, the forerunner of wine labelling.

From the climatic point of view, the island is divided into two distinct regions, one a hot, flat and sandy plain and the other more mountainous and cooled by the northern Aegean wind, the *meltemi*. Only wines produced on these northern slopes qualify for the Rhodos appellation. They include a dry white wine made from the Athiri grape and a pleasantly rounded red wine made from the Amorgiano variety.

In addition, there is Muscat of Rhodes, a sweet white dessert wine, which has its origins in ancient times. It is made from a blend of the white Muscat and the Trani Muscat grapes, which are cultivated to a limited extent in vineyards in the south of the island. I can testify that it is a superb wine to enjoy with a selection of *baklava* and *kataifi* pastries.

## CRETE

The history of Crete and the history of wines are as inextricably linked as the tendrils of a vine, and it is known that all the ancient centres of culture, including Knossos, Gortyns and Phaistos, enjoyed a flourishing wine trade. Beautifully decorated amphorae for the storage of wine were excavated at the Palace of Knossos, and in the centre of the island wine presses dating back to the seventeenth century BC have been discovered.

It is said that the island has the most traditional of all European vineyards, planted with old Cretan varieties whose origins elude the record books. To this day, the ungrafted vines produce a wide range of red and white wines, as well as sultanas and table grapes. The characteristic red wines of the island, which are renowned for their strong and full-bodied qualities, are traditionally made from the Romeiko grape strain from Hania, the Kotsifali from Heraklion and the Liatiko from the Lasithi Plain. The white wines of the island, which are made from old Cretan strains such as Vilana, Athiri and Ladikino, are known for their fruity taste and floral bouquet.

The island, sharply divided geographically and climatically by its huge mountain ranges, has four 'appellations of origin'. These have been granted to the Sitia vineyards in the extreme eastern corner of the island, where the Liatiko grape is planted up to a height of 600 metres (2,000 feet). This yields both a robust red wine and a fruity liqueur wine, which, if allowed to age, is enjoyed as an aperitif.

The same grape strain cultivated in the Daphnes region earns an appellation for wines of that name. Similar in character to the Sitia liqueur wine, they are reminiscent of the famous Malvasia wine, which, according to legend, was made in huge amphorae in the Minoan Palace from a recipe given by the Oracle of Delphi and said to symbolize wisdom. It will be recalled that it was in a butt of this wine, known in England as Malmsey, that the unfortunate Duke of Clarence reputedly drowned in 1478.

The two other Cretan appellations, Archanes and Peza, are both rich, ruby-red wines, full-bodied and with a pleasing bouquet. They are made from the Kotsifali vine, which is grown only around Heraklion, and the Mandelaria variety, which contributes the characteristic colour.

One of the largest wine-producing companies in Greece, D. Kourtakis S.A., has recently introduced two Cretan 'country wines', one red and one white, which represent a new status in Greek wines. The red wine, full-bodied and rounded, is blended from three local grape strains, Kotsifali, Liatiko and Mandelaria, and the white wine, which is delicate and crisp, comes from the Vilana grape.

## NORTHEAST AEGEAN ISLANDS

The principal wine-growing islands in the northeast Aegean are Samos and Lemnos, which market their wines, and Lesbos, which does not. Chios was a major producer, too, until its vineyards suffered the terrible fate lamented so vividly by Victor Hugo.

We turn to another poet, Lord Byron, for the

GREECE
& THE ISLANDS

ultimate accolade; he wrote: 'Fill high the cup with Samian wine.' The wine in question, which has its origins deep in the history of the island, is Muscat of Samos, the sweet white wine produced from the white Muscat grape, and the only one to earn the Samos appellation. It has a beautiful amber colour and is renowned for its mellow fruitiness and its pleasant, but not overwhelming sweetness. The wine is at its best served chilled, and it is ideal to sip as a leisurely accompaniment to an even sweeter Greek pastry.

The Muscat vineyard, which covers an area of 2,300 hectares (9 square miles), stretches between the two towns where the wine is made, Karlovassi and Samos, and is planted on narrow terraces rising from sea level to 800 metres (2,600 feet). A distinguishing local factor is the prolonged harvesting period, which begins in mid-August and is often not completed until October.

My own recollections of Samos wine are more earthy – of rich, dark red *mavros* wine (which means black and isn't all that inaccurate a description) made on a hillside farm and served with a succession of country casseroles – with goat, lamb, pork, everything.

Not to be outdone by its famous wine-growing neighbour, Lemnos, too, has an 'appellation' for its Muscat of Lemnos, made from the Muscat d'Alexandrie variety. One wine made from this grape is dry, fruity and fresh and has a subtle Muscat flavour; another, a liqueur wine, is smooth and mellow, with a beautiful old-gold colour and a powerful bouquet.

A grape grown on the island since ancient times – and mentioned by Aristotle, no less – is Limnia (or Limnio), which produces a clear, bright red wine said to be the colour of hot metal under the hammer of the god of fire and the forge, Hephaistos, the island's own deity.

## EVIA AND THE SPORADES

There are densely planted vineyards on Evia, mainly centred around Halkida and Karistos, where the Savatiano variety is grown, and on the Sporadic islands of Skyros and Skopelos. But the wines are little known outside the locality.

You may come across wine-making on a domestic scale, and in the most delightful way. I recall a hot and thirsty walk from the ferry port of Kimi, on the east coast of Evia, up into the hills; our destination was the convent of Sotiros. We rounded a corner and here, in a garden shaded by mulberry trees, were three members of a family treading red grapes in a tin bath, which is a messy business at the best of times. Our interruption was an excuse for a natural break, a friendly chat and a spot of refreshment, which finished up with all of us dancing *sirtaki* round and round the abandoned grape juice.

## CORFU AND THE IONIAN ISLANDS

The Ionian islands, which nestle close to the coastlines of mainland Greece and Albania, are characterized by a mild climate and a high rainfall.

Corfu produces good, dry, unresinated white wines and sweet, strong reds, of which, perhaps, Red Ropa is the most familiar to visitors. The island also produces the refreshing 'green' white wine, the beautifully clear Verdea, which is made to a greater extent on neighbouring Zakinthos (Zante) and Lefkas.

The Zakinthos vineyards are planted with a wide variety of grape strains, mostly white, while on Lefkas by far the greatest area is given over to the red Vertzami grape, which is grown on terraces colonizing steep slopes and gentle hillsides alike. This grape produces the powerful Santa Mavra wine (*mavra*, like *mavros*, means black), which is the pride of the island and is enjoyed – wine buffs please note – with everything from spit-roast lamb to fried fish.

The island of Cephallonia shares many of its climatic conditions with the nearby Peloponnese and has appellations to prove it. The white Robola grape, which is grown only in the mountainous regions of this island produces the fine, flinty, fruity white wine of the same name, Robola of Cephallonia. The other two accredited wines, both liqueur wines, are Muscat of Cephallonia and the red Mavrodaphne of Cephallonia, which is produced from the deep purple grape that is also grown extensively in Achaia.

# Cheese

It goes without saying – with all those herds of goats leaping about on the mountains, and flocks of woolly sheep lazing their time away in orchards – that most Greek cheeses are made from ewes' or goats' milk.

Cheese-making on the islands is still a thriving cottage industry, although there are, of course, dairies where cheese is made to traditional standards but using less time-honoured methods and equipment.

The tastiest cheese of your travels may be a slice of home-made *mizithra*, cut with a cotton thread and served in a cottage garden with a drizzle of *sirop* or honey or – a speciality of some Cretan villages – with a piece of cinnamon and orange bread; or it could be a slice of farmhouse feta cut from the block, sprinkled with olive oil and wild thyme flowers and offered with an ouzo and a bowl of olives.

## FETA
Perhaps the best-known of all Greek cheeses, feta is soft, white and crumbly, and with a pronounced 'bite' to it. It is made from ewes' milk, which is curdled with a starter such as buttermilk or rennet, and drained until it is firm. It is then heavily salted and packed into wooden barrels or large, square tins filled with whey. You come across it most often as a snack or as the essential ingredient in Greek country salads.

## MIZITHRA
Another traditional farmhouse product, this soft curd cheese is made of ewes' or goats' milk that has been boiled and diluted with water or whey. The milk is curdled with lemon juice, rennet or – a method which dates back to ancient times – the milky sap of the fig tree, which is introduced by stirring the liquid with a bruised twig. On Crete the cheese is drained overnight in flower-pot-shaped baskets lined with scalded cloths and is served at literally every meal of the day. I remember with particular affection a dish of pancakes we were offered

in a priest's house. They were filled almost to overflowing with *mizithra* and herbs, folded into half-moon shapes, deep fried in oil and served cold, liberally sprinkled with sugar and cinnamon. Mmm!

## ANTHOTIRO
A Cretan speciality, *anthotiro* is a soft, unsalted goats' cheese with a bland flavour that is much improved by the addition of a dollop of honey. The cheese is often served with fruit, especially grapes.

## GRAVIERA
A hard cheese, similar to gruyère, *graviera* is a good cooking cheese, and may be fried as *saganaki* (see page 80).

## KEFALOTIRI
The closest Greek cheese comes to Parmesan, *kefalotiri* takes its name from its wide, round shape, from *kefalo*, a hat. The cheese is very hard and very salty, and it has a tough rind. It is mainly used for cooking, especially where grated cheese is called for, but may also be cooked as *saganaki*. *Pinthos* is a type of *kefalotiri*.

## KASERI
A medium-hard cheese – another candidate for frying – *kaseri* has a mild flavour and is good for cooking, especially for sauces and toppings.

## KOPANISTI
Blue cheeses do not feature strongly in Greek output, so this one is something of a rarity. It is made from matured feta, which is allowed to develop a mould. This is then worked into the cheese, which has a sharp, peppery tang.

## PSILOTIRI
A local Cretan cheese, *psilotiri* is much sought-after by those who know it. It is made only from milk taken from goats grazed on the highest mountains (*psilo* means high); nothing else qualifies. A hard cheese with a very strong, clean flavour, it is served between courses to clear the palate.

# Vocabulary

## The Peloponnese and Saronic Gulf

| | |
|---|---|
| Country Bean Soup | *Φασόλια σούπα* |
| Octopus in Red Wine | *Χταπόδι κρασάτο* |
| Vine Leaf Parcels | *Ντολμαδάκια με ρύζι* |
| Lobster in Oil and Lemon Dressing | *Αστακός με σάλτσα λαδολέμονο* |
| Lamb Cooked with Lemons | *Αρνί λεμονάτο* |
| Red Mullet with Egg and Lemon Sauce | *Μπαρμπούνια αυγολέμονο* |
| Baked Sea Bream | *Συναγρίδα στο φούρνο* |
| Roast Chicken with Pistachios | *Κοτόπουλο γεμιστό με φιστίκια* |
| Sausage and Pepper Casserole | *Σπετζοφάϊ* |
| Doughnuts with Lemon Syrup | *Λουκουμάδες με σιρόπι* |
| Apricot Dessert | *Βερίκοκκο γλυκό* |

## The Cyclades

| | |
|---|---|
| Split Pea Purée | *Φάβα* |
| Fish Soup | *Κακαβιά* |
| Courgette Flower Fritters | *Τηγανητά άνθη κολοκυθιάς* |
| Cheese Pies | *Τυρόπιττες* |
| Baked Oysters | *Στρείδια στο φούρνο* |
| Potato Omelette | *Ομελέτα με πατάτες* |
| Goat and Haricot Casserole | *Κατσικάκι και φασόλια γιουβέτσι* |
| Braised Hare | *Λαγός στιφάδο* |
| Kithnos Honey and Cheese Pie | *Κυθνόπιττα* |
| Halva with Pistachios | *Χαλβάς με φιστίκια* |
| Rice Pudding | *Ρυζόγαλο* |

## The Dodecanese

| | |
|---|---|
| Baked Crab | *Κάβουρας στο φούρνο* |
| Prawns in Wine Sauce | *Γαρίδες κρασάτες* |
| Tuna with Garlic Sauce | *Τόννος με σκορδαλιά* |
| Mussel Pilaff | *Μύδια πιλάφι* |
| Roast Lamb with Quinces | *Αρνί ψητό με κυδώνια* |
| Lamb with Lettuce | *Αρνί με μαρούλια* |
| Chicken with Olives | *Κοτόπουλο με ελιές* |
| Veal Ragout | *Μοσχαράκι στιφάδο* |

| | |
|---|---|
| Partridge with Spaghetti | *Πέρδικες με σπαγέτο* |
| Pomegranates, Rhodes Style | *Ρόδια σε σιρόπι* |
| Apricot Preserve | *Βερίκοκκο γλυκό* |
| Quince Paste | *Κυδωνόπαστο* |

## Crete

| | |
|---|---|
| Pickled Artichoke Hearts | *Αγκινάρες τουρσί* |
| Prawn Pancakes | *Κροκέττες με γαρίδες* |
| Vineyard Fish | *Ψάρι με σταφύλια* |
| Fruit Plate | *Φρούτα της Κρήτης* |
| Squid, Rethymnon Style | *Καλαμαράκια Ρεθύμνου* |
| Lamb Cutlets in Paper | *Αρνίσια παϊδάκια στο χαρτί* |
| Pork with Celeriac | *Χοιρινό με σελινόριζες αυγολέμονο* |
| Chicken Breasts with Feta Cheese | *Κοτόπουλο με φέτα* |
| Rabbit, Knossos Style | *Κουνέλι Κνωσσού* |
| Mixed Vegetables in Egg and Lemon Sauce | *Λαχανικά ανάμιχτα αυγολέμονο* |
| Okra in Tomato Sauce | *Μπάμιες με σάλτσα ντομάτας* |
| Mixed Wild Greens | *Χόρτα ανάμιχτα* |
| Poached Apples | *Μήλα κρασάτα* |
| Katerina's Chocolate Cake | *Κέϊκ σοκολάτας της Κατερίνας* |

## The Northeast Aegean

| | |
|---|---|
| Rolled Courgette Flowers | *Γεμιστά άνφη κολοκυφιάς* |
| Fried Cheese | *Σαγανάκι* |
| Sardine Omelette | *Ομελέτα με σαρδέλλες* |
| Fried Squid with Garlic Sauce | *Καλαμαράκια τηγανητά με σκορδαλιά* |
| Steak with Thyme | *Φιλέτο με θυμάρι* |
| Fish Mayonnaise | *Ψάρι με μαγιονέζα* |
| Lemnos Veal | *Μοσχαράκι Λήμνου* |
| Beef with Courgettes | *Μοσχάρι με κολοκυθάκια* |
| Lamb and Macaroni Pie | *Παστίτσιο* |
| Chestnut Mountain | *Γλύκισμα με κάστανα* |
| Almond Pears | *Αμυγδαλωτά* |
| Sesame and Honey Toffee | *Παστέλι* |

| *Evia and Sporades* | |
|---|---|
| Pickled Octopus | Χταπόδι τουρσί |
| Cods' Roe Rissoles | Ταραμοκεφτέδες |
| Salt Cod with Courgettes | Μπακαλιάρος με κολοκυθάκια |
| Eel Soup | Χέλι σούπα |
| Fried Fish with Tomato Sauce | Ψάρια τηγανητά με σάλτσα ντομάτας |
| Pork Chops with Prunes | Χοιρινές ηπριζόλες με δαμάσκηνα |
| Stuffed Aubergines | Μελιτζάνες γεμιστές |
| Chicken with Cinnamon | Κοτόπουλο με κανέλλα |
| Custard Pies | Μπουγάτσες |
| Spinach Pie | Σπανακόπιττα |
| Easter Bread | Τσουρέκι |
| Fig and Walnut Dessert | Σύκα και καρύδια σε σιρόπι |

| *Corfu and Ionia* | |
|---|---|
| Chick-pea Purée | Χούμους |
| Grilled Fish with Garlic Sauce | Ψάρι με σκορδαλιά και αμύγδαλα |
| Fish Kebabs | Σουβλάκια ψαριού |
| Leg of Lamb with Pasta | Γιουβέτσι |
| Braised Beef | Στιφάδο |
| Chicken with Walnut Sauce | Κοτόπουλο με σάλτσα καρυδιού |
| Filo Custard Pie | Γαλακτομπούρεκο |
| Strawberries in Ouzo | Φράουλες με ούζο |
| Baked Quinces | Κυδώνια στο φούρνο |
| Walnut Biscuits | Κουραμπιέδες |
| Preserved Kumquats | Κουμκουάτ κουταλιού |
| Grape Juice Dessert | Μουσταλευριά |

# Acknowledgements

I should like to thank my husband, Douglas, and our friend Eric Bruton who have shared so many of my Greek island experiences; Evdokia Savani for her meticulous checking and friendly advice; and all the people on all the islands who so generously shared with me their traditional recipes and even their family secrets.

The publishers would like to thank the following photographers and organisations for their kind permission to reproduce the photographs in this book:

M. Couch 2–3, 6, 91 bottom, 130, 138–139; Frank Lane Picture Agency 94 Michael Clark, 131 top B. Borrell; National Tourist Organisation of Greece 10 and 11 N. Kontos, 18, 22, 23, 26, 27, 34–35 Y. Yiannopoulos, 39 E. Hard, 43, 50, 54 Randa Bishop, 54 bottom, 55, 59, 63, 70–71, 74 Y. Scouroyannis, 75, 79, 82, 83 Y. Scouroyannis, 90, 91 top, 95 A. Sofianopoulos, 102 top N. Kontos, 102 bottom, 106–107, 119 top E. Pap, 126. Douglas Westland 7, 39 bottom, 42, 62.

Special photography by Derek St Romaine © 14–15, 19, 30–31, 38, 46–47, 51, 58, 66–67, 78, 86–87, 98–99, 103, 110, 111, 114–115, 118, 119 bottom, 122, 123, 127.

Line drawings, colour illustrations and map by The Alternative Design Company, Devon

Thanks to:
Aristides Makris, Achaia Clauss S.A.; G. Zagrofistos, Archanes Wine, Crete; Leoni Sion, John Boutari & Son S.A.; Andrew Cambas, Cambas S.A.; Nikos Fragoulis and family, Paros; Graham L. Blake, D. Kourtakis S.A.; Nikos Kostopoulos and Aliki Katselis of National Tourist Organisation of Greece; J. Petridis, PLT(UK) Limited; Colin Deane, Porto Carras S.A.; T and R Adameos, Souvlia.

# Index

Page numbers in *italics* refer to captions to illustrations

**A**

Achaia 129, 136
Aegina 12, 20
Agia Galini 69
Agia Triada 59, 64
Ahivadolimni 33
Almond Pears 92
Alonissos 95, 108
Amarinthos 96
Amorgos 27, 37
Anafi 27, 41
Andimilos 27
Andros 27–8
*anthotiro* 137
Apricot Dessert 25
Apricot Preserve 57
Argolic plain 25
artichokes 7
    globe 7, 73
    Mixed Vegetables in Egg and
        Lemon Sauce 73
    pickled 7
    Pickled Artichoke Hearts 60
*artos* 21
Asklepion 48
Assumption, Feast of the 112
Astypalea 44
Aubergines, Stuffed 102, *102*
*avgolemona* 9

**B**

Baked Crab 44
Baked Oysters 33
Baked Quinces 122, *122*
Baked Sea Bream *18*, 20
bakeries 21
*baklava* 41
basil 25
Bassae 12
batter 32, 61
bay, sweet 101
beans
    Country Bean Soup 12
    Goat and Haricot Casserole
        36–7
    Mixed Vegetables in Egg and
        Lemon Sauce 73
beef
    Beef with Courgettes 88–9
    Braised Beef (*stifatho*) 116–17
Biscuits, Walnut (*kourambiedes*)
    124
*bougatses see* Custard Pies
Braised Beef (*stifatho*) 116–17
Braised Hare 37, *39*

bread 21, 29
    *artos* 21
    Easter Bread (*tsourekia*)
        108–109
    *lagana* 29
    wedding 21
Bream, Baked Sea *18*, 20
*briki* 93
butter
    parsley butter 33
    thyme butter 84

**C**

cake
    fig cake (*sikopitta*) 105
    Katerine's Chocolate Cake 77
    *vasilopita* 124
carrots
    Mixed Vegetables in Egg and
        Lemon Sauce 73
casseroles
    Goat and Haricot Casserole
        36–7
    Veal Ragout 52
Celeriac, Pork with 68–9
Cephallonia 112, 129, 136
chard 76
cheese 137
    *anthotiro* 137
    Cheese Pies (*tiropittes*)
        32–3, 43
    Chicken Breasts with Feta
        Cheese 69
    feta 32–3, 69, 137
    Fried Cheese (*saganaki*)
        80–81, 137
    *graviera* 137
    Honey and Cheese Pie 40
    *kaseri* 137
    *kefalotiri* 81, 137
    *kopanisti* 137
    *mizithra* 137
    *pinthos* 137
    *psilotiri* 137
    *xynogalo* 95
Chestnut Mountain 92
chicken 9
    Chicken Breasts with Feta
        Cheese 69
    Chicken with Cinnamon 104
    Chicken with Olives 50, *50*
    Chicken with Walnut Sauce
        117
    Roast Chicken with
        Pistachios 20–21
Chick-pea Purée 112
Chios (Hios) 79, 82, 133
Chocolate Cake, Katerine's 77
Cinnamon, Chicken with 104

'Clean Monday' *see Kathari
    Deftera*
cod
    Cods' Roe Rissoles
        (*taramokeftethes*) 96–7
    Salt Cod with Courgettes
        98–9, *99*
coffee 93
Corfu 49, 85, 111–25, 127–8
    wines 129, 136
Corinth 12, 13
Cos 48, 50
Country Bean Soup 12
courgette flowers
    Courgette Flower Fritters 32
    Rolled Courgette Flowers 80
courgettes
    Beef with Courgettes 88–9
    Salt Cod with Courgettes
        98–9, *99*
Crab, Baked 44
Crete 59–77, 129
    wines 133
Custard Pies 104–105, *111*
    Filo Custard Pie 120
Cyclades 27–41
    wines 132–3

**D**

dandelion leaves 76
Daphnes region 133
Delphi, Oracle of 133
Demesthika 132
Desserts
    Almond Pears 92
    Apricot Dessert 25
    Baked Quinces 122, *122*
    Chestnut Mountain 92
    Custard Pies 104–105
    Doughnuts with Lemon
        Syrup 24–5
    Fig and Walnut Dessert 109
    Filo Custard Pie *111*, 120
    Grape Juice Dessert 125
    Poached Apples 77
    Pomegranates, Rhodes
        Style 53
    Rice Pudding 41
    Sesame and Honey Toffee 93
    Strawberries in Ouzo 120–21
Diafani 43
Dinner of Love 47
Dionysos 27, 129
Dodecanese 43–57
    wines 133
Dormiton Day 112
doughnuts 41
    Doughnuts with Lemon
        Syrup 24–5

**E**

Easter 65, 109, 127–8
    eggs (*kokkina avga*) 108, 109,
        127
Easter Bread (*tsoureki*) 108–109
Eel Soup 100
eggs
    Easter (*kokkina avga*) 108, 109,
        127
    Mixed Vegetables in Egg and
        Lemon Sauce 73
    Potato and Sausage Omelette
        (*froutalia*) 36
    Red Mullet with Egg and
        Lemon Sauce 17
    Sardine Omelette 81
Epidavros 11
Ermoupolis 40
Euripides 11
Evia 95–109, 129
    wines 136

**F**

fennel 69
    Mixed Vegetables in Egg and
        Lemon Sauce 73
feta cheese 32–3, 137
    Chicken Breasts with Feta
        Cheese 69
figs 105, *119*
    Fig and Walnut Dessert 109
    fig cake (*sikopitta*) 105
Filo Custard Pie *111*, 120
filo pastry 33, 120, 121
fish *see* seafood
Fish Kebabs 114, *114*
Fish Mayonnaise 8, *79*, 84–5
Fish Soup (*kakavia*) 8, 28–9, *32*,
    33
fish stock 17, 29, 100
Folegandros 27
Fried Cheese (*saganaki*) 80–81,
    137
Fried Fish with Tomato Sauce
    100–101
Fried Squid with Garlic Sauce
    82
*froutalia see* Potato and Sausage
    Omelette
fruit
    Almond Pears 92
    Apricot Dessert 25
    Apricot Preserve 57
    Baked Quinces 122, *122*
    Fruit Plate 64
    Grape Juice Dessert 125
    Poached Apples 77
    Pomegranates,
        Rhodes Style 53

Preserved Kumquats 125
Quince Paste 57
Roast Lamb with Quinces 48
Strawberries in Ouzo *119*,
120–21
*see also* prickly pears

**G**

game 8–9
Braised Hare 37, *39*
Partridge with Spaghetti
52–3
Rabbit, Knossos Style 72
garlic sauce 82
garlic and almond sauce 113
*skorthalia* 45, 61, 113
globe artichokes *see* artichokes
goat 9, 80
Goat and Haricot
Casserole 36–7
Pascal goat 127, 128
Good Friday 65
Gortyns 133
Grape Juice Dessert 125
*graviera* 137
Greens, Mixed Wild 76, 108
Grilled Fish with Garlic Sauce
112–13

**H**

Halkida 136
Halva with Pistachios 40–41
Hania 133
Hare, Braised 37, *39*
Heracles' blood 13
Heraklion 133
herbs
basil 25
bay 101
oregano (Cretan dittany) 73
parsley butter 33
rosemary 53
sage 113
sweet bay 101
thyme 73, 80, 81, *91*
thyme butter 84
thyme flowers 20, 21, 84
Hios *see* Chios
Homer 132
honey 41
Honey and Cheese Pie 40
rosemary 53
Sesame and Honey Toffee 93
Hora (Patmos) 52
Hora (Skyros) 96, 104
*horiatikisalata* 9, 85
Hydra 12, 16

**I**

Ierapetra 61
Ikaria 79, 80, 92
Ionia 111–25
wines 136
Ithaca 112

**K**

*kafenion* 8, 63, 93, 97
*kakavia see* Fish Soup
*kalamares see* squid
Kalamata 24, 49
olives 11, 49
*kalamatianos* 24
Kalavrita 16
Kalymnos 44, 47
Kamiros 53
karistos 136
*karithia* 95
Karlovassi 136
Karpathos 43, *43*, 48, 57
*kaseri* 137
*kataifi* 41
Katerina's Chocolate Cake 77
*Kathari Deftera* ('Clean
Monday') 29, 65
Kea 27
Kebabs, Fish 114, *114*
*kefalotiri* 81, 137
Kerkira 127–8, *127*
Kithnos 40
Klima 33
Knossos 133
*kokkina avga* (Easter eggs) 108,
109, 127
*kokoretsi* 11
*kopanisti* 137
Kos 44
*koumaria* 79
*kourambiedes see* Walnut Biscuits
*kritharaki* 104
Kumquats, Preserved 9, 125
*see also* 'spoon sweets'

**L**

*lagana* 29
Lakki 68
lamb 9
Lamb and Macaroni Pie
(pastitsio) 7, 89
Lamb Cooked with Lemons
16–17
Lamb Cutlets in Paper 68, *68*
Lamb with Lettuce 48–9
Leg of Lamb with Pasta
(*yiouvetsi*) 116
Pascal lamb 127, 128
Roast Lamb with Quinces 48
Lasithi Plain 59, 133
Lefkas 41, 112, 129, 136
Leg of Lamb with Pasta
(*yiouvetsi*) 116
Lemnos (Limnos) 8, 79, 84, 93,
133, 136
Lemnos Veal 88, *88*
Lent 29, 65, 127
Lesbos 79, 133
Lettuce, Lamb with 48–9
Liapades 111
Limnos *see* Lemnos
Lobster in Oil and Lemon
Dressing 16

**M**

mackerel 100
*magiritsa* 128
Mani 11–12
marinades 37, 114
mastic 82
*mavros* wine 37, 136
May, First of *see Protomayia*
mayonnaises 84–5
Fish Mayonnaise 8, *79*, 84–5
meat 8–9
Beef with Courgettes 88–9
Braised Beef (*stifatho*)
116–117
Braised Hare 37, *39*
Goat and Haricot Casserole
36–7
Lamb and Macaroni Pie
(*pastitsio*) 7, 89
Lamb Cooked with Lemons
16–17
Lamb Cutlets in Paper 68, *68*
Lamb with Lettuce 48–9
Lemnos Veal 88, *88*
Leg of Lamb with Pasta
(*yiouvetsi*) 116
Pork Chops with Prunes 101
Pork with Celeriac 68–9
Roast Lamb with Quinces 48
Steak with Thyme 84
Veal Ragout 52
*see also* sausages
Messinia 11, 12
Methoni 132
*mezethakia* 9, 97
Mikonos 27
Milos 27, 33
*mistelle* 133
Mixed Vegetables in Egg and
Lemon Sauce 73
Mixed Wild Greens 76, 108
*mizithra* 137
Monemvassia 17
mullet 29
Red Mullet with Egg and
Lemon Sauce 17
Mussel Pilaff 47, *47*
Mycenae 11

**N**

Naxos 27
Nemean wine 13, 132
New Year's Eve 124
Nissyros 44, 52
Northeast Aegean islands 79–93
wines 133–6

**O**

octopus 29
cleaning 13
Octopus in Red Wine 12–13
Pickled Octopus 96
Okra in Tomato Sauce 76
Olimbos 43
olive oil 85

olives 11, 49
Chicken with Olives 50, *50*
Kalamata 11, 49
*throumbes* 49
Olympia 11
omelettes
Potato and Sausage Omelette
(*froutalia*) 36
Sardine Omelette 81
*ouzaria* 97
ouzo 97, 132
Strawberries in Ouzo *119*,
120–21
Oysters, Baked 33

**P**

Pancakes, Prawn (*crockettes*) *59*,
61
Paralia Kimi 95
Paros 8, 27, *39*, 129, 132, 133
parsley butter 33
Partridge with Spaghetti 52–3
Pascal goat or lamb 127, 128
pasta
*kritharaki* 104
Lamb and Macaroni Pie
(*pastitsio*) 7, 89
Leg of Lamb with Pasta
(*yiouvetsi*) 116
Partridge with Spaghetti
52–3
*pastitsio see* Lamb and Macaroni
Pie
Patmos 52
Patra 132
Paxos 112
Pears, Almond 92
Peloponnese 11–25, 49
wines 132
peppers
Sausage and Pepper
Casserole 24
Phaistos 59, 64, 133
Pickled Aritchoke Hearts 60
Pickled Octopus 96
pies
Cheese Pies (*tiropittes*) 32–3,
43
Custard Pies 104–105
Filo Custard Pie *111*, 120
Honey and Cheese Pie 40
Lamb and Macaroni Pie
(*pastitsio*) 7
Spinach Pie 108
Pigathia 43
*pinthos* 137
Piraeus 43
pistachios
Halva with Pistachios 40–41
Roast Chicken with
Pistachios 20–21
Poached Apples 77
Pomegranates, Rhodes Style 53
pork
Pork Chops with Prunes 101
Pork with Celeriac 68–9

Poros 12
potatoes
    Mixed Vegetables in Egg and
        Lemon Sauce 73
    Potato and Sausage Omelette
        (*froutalia*) 36
poultry 9
    Chicken Breasts with Feta
        Cheese 69
    Chicken with Cinnamon 104
    Chicken with Olives 50, *50*
    Chicken with Walnut Sauce
        117
    Partridge with Spaghetti
        52–3
    Roast Chicken with
        Pistachios 20–21
prawns 29
    Prawn Pancakes (*crockettes*)
        *59*, 61
    Prawns in Wine Sauce 44–5
preserves
    Apricot Preserve 57
    Preserved Kumquats 125
prickly pears 57
*Protomayia* 72, 113, *119*
Prunes, Pork Chops with 101
*psilotiri* 137
purées
    Chick-pea Purée 112
    Split Pea Purée 28


Q

quinces
    Baked Quinces 122, *122*
    Quince Paste 57
    Roast Lamb with Quinces 48


R

Rabbit, Knossos Style 72
*raki* (*tsipouro*) 61
red mullet 29
    Red Mullet with Egg and
        Lemon Sauce 17
retsina 20, 130–32
Rhodes 43, *43*, 53, 57, 129, 133
Rice Pudding 41
Rissoles, Cods' Roe
    (*taramokeftethes*) 96–7
Roast Lamb with Quinces 48
Rolled Courgette Flowers 80
rosemary 53


S

*saganaki see* Fried Cheese
sage 113
St Demetrius' Day 131
salads 9, 85, 98
Salamis 12
Samian wine 80, 136
Samos 49, 79, 129, 133, 136
Samothrace 79
Santorini (Thera, Thira) 28, *39*,
    129, 132

Sardine Omelette 81
Saronic Gulf 11–25
sauces and dressings
    egg and lemon sauce 17, 73
    garlic sauce (*skorthalia*) 45,
        61, 113
    garlic (with potato) sauce 82
    garlic and almond sauce 113
    oil and lemon dressing 16
    tomato sauce 76, 100–101
    walnut sauce 117
    wine sauce 44–5
    yoghurt sauce 88, 102
sausages
    *kokoretsi* 11
    Potato and Sausage Omelette
        (*froutalia*) 36
    Sausage and Pepper
        Casserole 24
sea bream
    Baked Sea Bream *18*, 20
    Vineyard Fish 64
seafood 7–8, 29
    Baked  Crab 44
    Baked Oysters 33
    Baked Sea Bream *18*, 20
    Cods' Roe Rissoles
        (*taramokeftethes*) 96–7
    Eel Soup 100
    Fish Kebabs 114, *114*
    Fish Mayonnaise 8, *9*, 84–5
    Fish Soup (*kakavia*) 8, 28–9,
        *32*, 33
    fish stock 17, 29, 100
    Fried Fish with Tomato
        Sauce 100–101
    Fried Squid with Garlic
        Sauce 82
    Grilled Fish with Garlic
        Sauce 112–13
    Lobster in Oil and Lemon
        Dressing 16
    Mussel Pilaff 47, *47*
    Octopus in Red Wine 12–13
    Pickled Octopus 96
    Prawn Pancakes (*crockettes*)
        *59*, 61
    Prawns in Wine Sauce 44–5
    Red Mullet with Egg and
        Lemon Sauce 17
    Salt Cod with Courgettes
        98–9, *99*
    Sardine Omelette 81
    Squid, Rethymnon Style 65
    Tuna with Garlic Sauce 45
    Vineyard Fish 64
Sesame and Honey Toffee 93
*sesfikia* 95
shellfish *see* seafood
shrimps 29
*siko glyko* 105
*sikopitta* 105
Siphnos 27, 36, *36*
Siros 40
Skiathos 95–6
Skopelos 95, 101, 136
*skorthalia see* garlic sauce

Skyros 95, 96, 104, 136
sorrel 76
soups
    Country Bean Soup 12
    Eel Soup 100
    Fish Soup (*kakavia*) 8, 28–9,
        *32*, 33
    *magiritsa* 128
Spaghetti, Partridge with 52–3
Spetsai (Spetses) 12, 20
spinach 76
    Spinach Pie 108
Split Pea Purée 28
'spoon sweets' 9, 125
Sporades 49, 95–109
    wines 136
squid (*kalamares*) 29
    Fried Squid with Garlic
        Sauce 82
    Squid, Rethymnon Style 65
Stavros Day 25
Steak with Thyme 84
*stefani* 72, *95*, *119*
*stifatho see* Braised Beef
stock, fish 17, 29, 100
Strawberries in Ouzo *119*,
    120–21
Stuffed Aubergines 102, *102*
sweet bay 101
Symi 44–5


T

*taramokeftethes see* Cods' Roe
    Rissoles
tavernas 62–3
Thassos 49, 79, 92, 129
Theophrastus 73
Thera, Thira *see* Santorini
Thronos 73
*throumbes* 49
thyme 73, 80, 81, *91*
    Steak with Thyme 84
thyme butter 84
thyme flowers 20, 21, 84
Tilissos 59
Tinos 27
*tiropittes see* Cheese Pies
Toffee, Sesame and Honey 93
tomatoes
    Fried Fish with Tomato
        Sauce 100–101
    Okra in Tomato Sauce 76
*tsipouro see* raki
*tsoureki see* Easter bread
Tuna with Garlic Sauce 45


V

Vai 77
Valanion 111
*vasilopitta* 124
veal
    Lemnos Veal 88, *88*
    Veal Ragout 52
vegetables 9
    Chick-pea Purée 112

Country Bean Soup 12
Courgette Flower Fritters 32
Mixed Vegetables in Egg and
    Lemon Sauce 73
Mixed Wild Greens 76, 108
Okra in Tomato Sauce 76
Pickled Artichoke Hearts 60
Rolled Courgette Flowers 80
Spinach Pie 108
Split Pea Purée 28
Stuffed Aubergines 102, *102*
Vine Leaf Parcels 13, *16*
vermouth 133
Vine Leaf Parcels 13, *16*
Vineyard Fish 64


W

walnuts 95
    Walnut Biscuits
        (*kourambiedes*) 124
    Chicken with Walnut Sauce
        117
    Fig and Walnut Dessert 109
wedding breads 21
Wild Greens, Mixed 76, 108
wine
    Octopus in Red Wine 12–13
    Prawns in Wine Sauce 44–5
wines 129–36, *134–5*
    grand reserve (*eithika
        epilegmenos*) wines 130
    home-made wine 77
    *mavros* 37, 136
    *mistelle* 133
    reserve (*epilegmenos*) wines
        130
    retsina 20, 130–32
    'table wines' 130
    *see also* ouzo, *raki*
wreaths *see stefani*


X

*xynogalo* 95


Y

*yemistes* 102
*yiouvetsi see* Leg of Lamb with
    Pasta
yoghurt 56
    sauce 88, 102
    stabilizing 89
*ypovrychion* 82


Z

*zacharoplasteion* 63
Zakinthos (Zante) 112, 117, 129,
    136